Gold Stars

FIFTH GRADE MATH WORKBOOK

Parragon

Helping Your Child

- Remember that the activities in this book should be enjoyed by your child. Try to find a quiet place to work.
- Always give your child lots of encouragement and praise.
- Your child does not need to complete each page in one sitting. Always stop before your child grows tired, and come back to the same page another time.
- Be sure to do the activities in the order they appear in the book because they increase in difficulty.
- The answers to the activities are on pages 91–96.

5005 Newport Drive, Rolling Meadows, Illinois 60008

Written by Nina Filipek
Cover art by Katie Melrose
Illustrated by Simon Abbott, Adam Linley, and Helen Prole
Educational Consultant: Maria Luce

ISBN: 979-8-89019-076-5

Contents

Decimal Numbers Place Value

A decimal is a part of a whole number. Notice that the decimal point separates the whole number from the part of a number.
Write these decimal numbers in the place value chart below.
The first one is done for you.

0.15 0.015 0.7 7.1 10.05 110.005

Hundreds	Tens	Units		Tenths	Hundredths	Thousandths
		0	.	1	5	

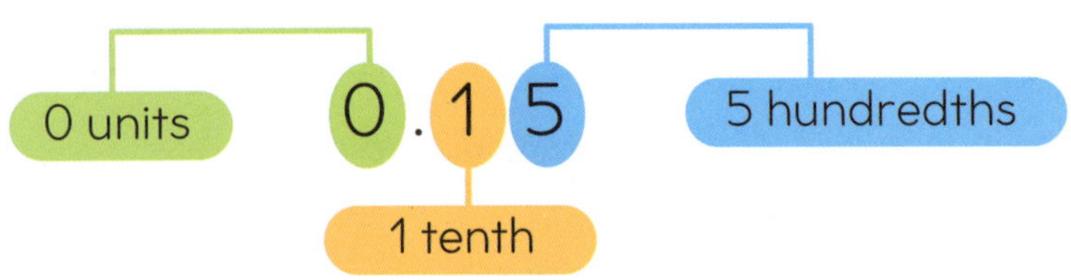

0.15 as a fraction

$$= \frac{1}{10} + \frac{5}{100}$$

How do we say 0.15? We can say: "one tenth and five hundredths" or we can say "fifteen hundredths" because $(\frac{1}{10} = \frac{10}{100}) + \frac{5}{100} = \frac{15}{100}$.

How do we say 0.015? We can say "one hundredth and five thousandths" or "fifteen thousandths" because $(\frac{1}{100} = \frac{10}{1,000}) + \frac{5}{1,000} = \frac{15}{1,000}$.

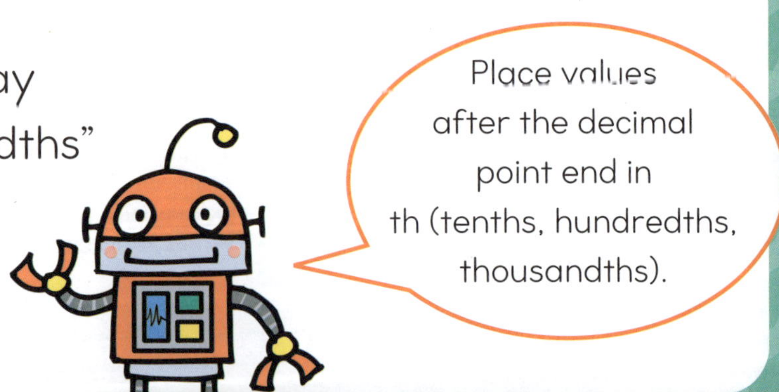

Note for parent: After the decimal point, the first digit represents tenths, the second digit hundredths, and the third digit thousandths.

Comparing Decimals

Which is greater 1.352 or 1.320?

1.352: 1 unit, $\frac{3}{10}$, $\frac{5}{100}$, $\frac{2}{1,000}$

1.320: 1 unit, $\frac{3}{10}$, $\frac{2}{100}$, $\frac{0}{1,000}$

Follow these steps to find out.

Step 1: Start from the left of each number and compare the whole units before the decimal points. Both are 1 unit so no difference here.

Step 2: Move to the right to compare the tenths after the decimal points. 1.352 has $\frac{3}{10}$ and 1.320 also has $\frac{3}{10}$. So no difference here.

Step 3: Move to the right to compare the hundredths. 1.352 has $\frac{5}{100}$ and 1.320 has $\frac{2}{100}$ so 1.350 is greater than 1.320. We don't need to look at the thousandths because these are 10 times smaller than hundredths.

We can write this as: 1.352 > 1.320

Remember the signs: **>** greater than **<** less than **=** equal

Which is greater 0.7 or 0.07?

0.7: 0 units, $\frac{7}{10}$

0.07: 0 units, $\frac{0}{10}$, $\frac{7}{100}$

$\frac{7}{10}$ is greater than $\frac{7}{100}$ because tenths are 10 times greater than hundredths.

0.7 [ ] 0.07

Which is greater?
Write the signs in the boxes.

0.15 [ ] 0.015

0.8 [ ] 0.80

0.25 [ ] 0.255

0.99 [ ] 1.9

0.091 [ ] 1.901

Note for parent: Children need to remember that 1 tenth is 10 times greater than 1 hundredth, and 1 hundredth is 10 times greater than 1 thousandth.

Expanding Decimals

As with other numbers, we can write decimals in expanded form.

3.5

$= \underbrace{(3 \times 1)} + \underbrace{(5 \times \frac{1}{10})}$

$= 3 \text{ units} + \frac{5}{10}$

$= 3 + \frac{5}{10}$

32.54

$= \underbrace{(3 \times 10)} + \underbrace{(2 \times 1)} + \underbrace{(5 \times \frac{1}{10})} + \underbrace{(4 \times \frac{1}{100})}$

$= 3 \text{ tens} + 2 \text{ units} + \frac{5}{10} + \frac{4}{100}$

$= 30 + 2 + \frac{5}{10} + \frac{4}{100}$

Try expanding these decimals for yourself.

1. $7.2 = (7 \times 1) + (2 \times \frac{\square}{\square})$

2. $9.6 = (9 \times 1) + (6 \times \frac{\square}{\square})$

3. $8.63 = (8 \times 1) + (6 \times \frac{\square}{\square}) + (3 \times \frac{\square}{\square})$

4. $16.4 = (1 \times \square) + (6 \times \square) + (4 \times \frac{\square}{\square})$

5. $45.02 = (4 \times \square) + (5 \times \square) + (2 \times \frac{\square}{\square})$

Note: Writing the numbers in a place value chart can help you see the value of each of the digits.

Hundreds	Tens	Units		Tenths	Hundredths	Thousandths
	4	5	.	0	2	

Note for parent: Using a place value chart will help your child visualize the value of each digit in the number.

Look at how this larger number can be expanded.

347.392

$= (3 \times 100) + (4 \times 10) + (7 \times 1) + (3 \times \frac{1}{10}) + (9 \times \frac{1}{100}) + (2 \times \frac{1}{1{,}000})$

$= 3$ hundreds $+ 4$ tens $+ 7$ units $+ \frac{3}{10} + \frac{9}{100} + \frac{2}{1{,}000}$

$= 300 + 40 + 7 + \frac{3}{10} + \frac{9}{100} + \frac{2}{1{,}000}$

Here are some more for you to try:

1. $72.803 = (7 \times \square) + (2 \times 1) + (8 \times \frac{\square}{\square}) + (3 \times \frac{\square}{\square})$

2. $530.903 = (5 \times 100) + (3 \times \square) + (9 \times \frac{\square}{\square}) + (3 \times \frac{\square}{\square})$

3. $702.56 = (7 \times \square) + (2 \times 1) + (5 \times \frac{\square}{\square}) + (6 \times \frac{\square}{\square})$

Let's try the reverse and write the standard decimal form from the expanded numbers.

4. $(7 \times 10) + (7 \times \frac{1}{10}) + (5 \times \frac{1}{100}) = \square$

5. $(5 \times 10) + (3 \times 1) + (4 \times \frac{1}{10}) = \square$

6. $(6 \times 100) + (8 \times 10) + (3 \times \frac{1}{10}) + (2 \times \frac{1}{1{,}000}) = \square$

Multiply by Powers of 10

When we multiply 5 by 10 we move the 5 digit into the tens place by putting a zero on the end of the number as a placeholder. When we multiply by 100 we move the 5 into the hundreds place and put two zeros at the end. Can you see a pattern forming?

Th	H	T	U	
			5	
		5	0	→ 5 x 10
	5	0	0	→ 5 x 100 or 50 x 10
5,	0	0	0	→ 5 x 1,000 or 500 x 10

50 is 10 times greater than 5

Look for patterns when you multiply these numbers.

3 x 10 = ______ 7 x 10 = ______

30 x 10 = ______ 70 x 10 = ______

300 x 10 = ______ 700 x 10 = ______

Try these:

42 x 10 = ______ 136 x 10 = ______

42 x 100 = ______ 136 x 100 = ______

42 x 1,000 = ______ 136 x 1,000 = ______

Note to parent: This activity helps children understand why we add a zero to the end of a number when we multiply by 10, and what this zero means.

Divide by Powers of 10

When we divide 5,000 by 10 we move the 5 digit into the hundreds place and lose a zero at the end of the number. When we divide by 100 we move the 5 into the tens place and lose two zeros at the end. Can you see a pattern forming?

Th	H	T	U	
5,	0	0	0	
	5	0	0	→ 5,000 ÷ 10
		5	0	→ 500 ÷ 10
			5	→ 50 ÷ 10

500 is 10 times less than 5,000

Look for patterns when you multiply these numbers.

30 ÷ 10 =

300 ÷ 10 =

3,000 ÷ 10 =

70 ÷ 10 =

700 ÷ 10 =

7,000 ÷ 10 =

Try these:

650 ÷ 10 =

6,500 ÷ 100 =

65,000 ÷ 1,000 =

1,460 ÷ 10 =

14,600 ÷ 100 =

146,000 ÷ 1,000 =

Note for parent: This activity helps children understand why we lose a zero at the end of a number when we divide by 10, and what this means.

Exponents

What is an **exponent**?
An exponent is also known as a "power." It tells us how many times we multiply a base number by itself.

10^2

10 is the base number

2 is the exponent

$10^2 = 10 \times 10 = 100$

- 10^2 — exponential form
- 10×10 — expanded form
- 100 — standard form

When referring to 10^2 we can say, "10 to the power of 2," or "10 squared."

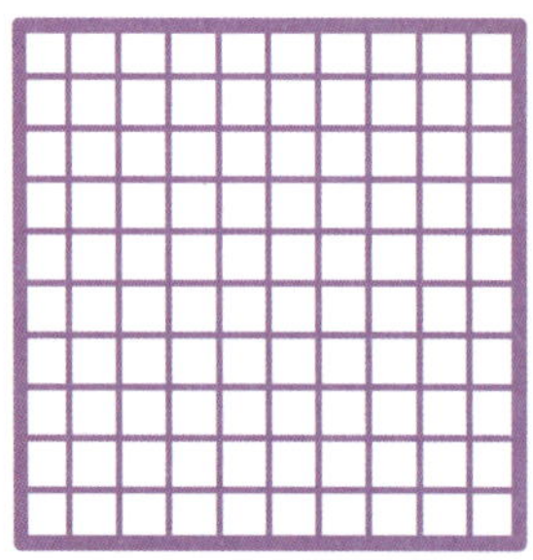

$10^2 = 100$

When we multiply a whole number by itself the product is called a "square number."

$1 \times 1 = 1$, $2 \times 2 = 4$, $3 \times 3 = 9$, $4 \times 4 = 16$, $5 \times 5 = 25$, and so on. The products 1, 4, 9, 16, and 25 are square numbers.

1 x 1 2 x 2 3 x 3

$$10^3 = 10 \times 10 \times 10$$
$$= 100 \times 10$$
$$= 1{,}000$$

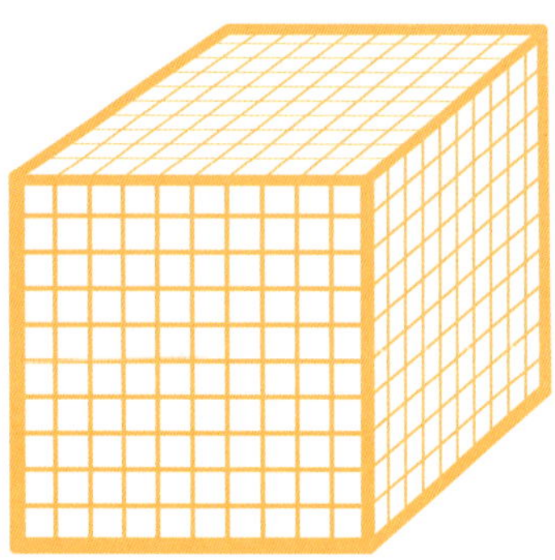

For 10^3 we say, "10 to the power of 3," or "10 cubed" because this number looks like a cube.

$10^3 = 1{,}000$

The products of these multiplications are cube numbers:
$1 \times 1 \times 1 = 1$, $2 \times 2 \times 2 = 8$, $3 \times 3 \times 3 = 27$, $4 \times 4 \times 4 = 64$, $5 \times 5 \times 5 = 125$.

1 x 1 x 1 2 x 2 x 2 3 x 3 x 3

Note for parent: It is a common mistake for children to think that $10^2 = 10 \times 2$. They will need reminding of this error because $10^2 = 10 \times 10$.

Figure out the products. Can you see a pattern forming?

$10^1 = 10$

$10^2 = 10 \times 10 =$ ....

$10^3 = 10 \times 10 \times 10$

$= 100 \times 10 =$ ....

$10^4 = 10 \times 10 \times 10 \times 10$

$=$ .... $\times 10 =$ ....

$10^5 = 10 \times 10 \times 10 \times 10 \times 10$

$=$ .... $\times 10 =$ ....

$10^6 = 10 \times 10 \times 10 \times 10 \times 10 \times 10$

$=$ .... $\times 10 =$ ....

Put in commas to separate thousands by starting from the last digit in the number and counting backward in threes.

1 2	1 2 3	1 2 3 4	1 2 3 4 5	1 2 3 4 5 6
$10^2 = 100$	$10^3 = 1{,}000$	$10^4 = 10{,}000$	$10^5 = 100{,}000$	$10^6 = 1{,}000{,}000$
2 zeros	☐ zeros	☐ zeros	☐ zeros	☐ zeros

Write the expanded form then figure out the product.

$10^7 = 10 \times 10 \times 10 \times 10 \times 10 \times 10 \times 10 =$ ....

$10^8 =$ ....

$10^9 =$ ....

$10^{10} =$ ....

Multi-Digit Multiplication

Find the product of these multi-digit numbers.
Study the example below.

295 x 15 =

Th	H	T	U
	4	2	
	2	9	5
x		1	5
1,	4	7	5
2,	9	5	0
4,	4	2	5

x	200	90	5		
10	2,000	900	50	=	2,950
5	1,000	450	25	=	1,475
				=	4,425

Step 1: Multiply by 5 units. Carry over 2 tens. Carry over 4 hundreds.

Step 2: Put 0 as a placeholder before multiplying by 1 ten.

Step 3: Add the products of Step 1 and Step 2.

Here are some multiplication problems for you to try.

546 x 26 =

Th	H	T	U
	5	4	6
x		2	6

x	500	40	6		
20				=	
6				=	
				=	

Step 1: Multiply by 6 units. Carry over any tens or hundreds.

Step 2: Put 0 as a placeholder before multiplying by 2 tens.

Step 3: Add the products of Step 1 and Step 2.

Note for parent: Different methods of multiplication are used here to help develop children's math skills and understanding.

427 x 35 =

	Th	H	T	U
		4	2	7
x			3	5

x	400	20	7		
30				=	
5				=	
				=	

Step 1: Multiply by 5 units. Carry over any tens or hundreds.

Step 2: Put 0 as a placeholder before multiplying by 3 tens.

Step 3: Add the products of Step 1 and Step 2.

625 x 43 =

	Th	H	T	U
		6	2	5
x			4	3

x	600	20	5		
40				=	
3				=	
				=	

Step 1: Multiply by 3 units. Carry over any tens or hundreds.

Step 2: Put 0 as a placeholder before multiplying by 4 tens.

Step 3: Add the products of Step 1 and Step 2.

505 X 26 =

	Th	H	T	U
		5	0	5
x			2	6

x	500	0	5		
20				=	
6				=	
				=	

Step 1: Multiply by 6 units. Carry over any tens or hundreds.

Step 2: Put 0 as a placeholder before multiplying by 2 tens.

Step 3: Add the products of Step 1 and Step 2.

Multi-Digit Division—Area Models

Suppose you wanted to find out the answer to this problem: **If you saved $35 per month, how long would it take you to buy a guitar that costs $735?** You could write this problem as **735 ÷ 35** and use an area model to find the answer.

Step 1: Figure out some useful multiples of the divisor.

35 x 2 = 70

35 x 10 = 350

35 x 20 = 700

Step 2: After 10 months you have saved $350 and after 20 months $700.

Step 3: You need to save for one more month.

x	10	10	1
35	350	350	35

735	385	35
− 350	− 350	− 35
385	35	0

Step 4: In total, you need to save for 21 months to buy the guitar.

If 484 stickers are shared equally between 22 children, how many stickers would each child get? This problem could be written as **484 ÷ 22**. Complete the area model.

Useful multiples:

22 x 2 = ...

22 x 10 = ...

22 x 20 = ...

x	20	2
22	440	

484	
− 440	−
44	

Answer: Each child gets ☐ stickers.

Note for parent: Children can use different factors with area models. However, many children will find it easier to subtract from the total in groups of ten.

630 children are going to school by minibus. If each minibus can take 15 passengers, how many minibuses will be needed?

This problem could be written as: ☐ ÷ ☐ .

Complete the area model.

Useful multiples:

15 x 2 = ...

15 x 10 = ...

15 x 20 = ...

15 x 40 = ...

x	40	2
15	600	

630

— ______ — ______

....

Answer: ☐ minibuses will be needed.

552 people are sitting in a movie theater in equal rows of 24 people. How many rows of people are there?

This problem could be written as: ☐ ÷ ☐ .

Complete the area model.

Useful multiples:

24 x 2 = ...

24 x 10 = ...

24 x 20 = ...

x	20	2	1
24	480		

552

— ______ — ______ — ______

....

Answer: There are ☐ rows of people.

Multiply Decimals by Powers of Ten

Placing zeros at the end of the number doesn't work when we multiply decimals. We need to move the decimal point to the right to increase the value of the number.

✗ 4.2 x 10 = 4.20 is wrong because the number is still the same value

✓ 4.2 x 10 = 42 is correct because 42 is 10 times greater than 4.2

The arrows below show you the decimal moves one place to the right when we multiply by 10 and two places to the right when we multiply by 100.

1.5 x 10 = 15

1 . 5

Or we can write 15.0 as a decimal number.

1.5 x 100 = 150

1 . 5 0

Or we can write 150.0 as a decimal number.

Circle the correct products for these decimal multiplication problems.

1. 2.5 x 10 = 250 or 25
2. 0.5 x 10 = 50 or 5
3. 17.5 x 10 = 175 or 1,750
4. 5.6 x 100 = 560 or 56
5. 1.8 x 100 = 1,800 or 180
6. 42.15 x 100 = 4,215 or 42,150

If you are unsure of your answer, there is a quick way of checking. Look at the last problem as an example.

Step 1: Find the nearest whole number to the decimal. The nearest whole number to 42.15 is 42.

Step 2: Multiply 42 by 100. The answer is 4,200. So a reasonable answer will be close to this number.

Step 3: Choose between 4,215 or 42,150. The answer must be 4,215!

Note for parent: This activity helps children understand that when we move a decimal point to the right we are increasing the value of the number.

When we multiply by 1,000 we move the decimal three places to the right.

1.5 x 1,000 = 1,500

1 . 5 0 0

Or we can write 1,500.0 as a decimal number.

When we multiply by 1,000 it is like multiplying by 10 three times.
1.5 x 10 = 15
15 x 10 = 150
150 x 10 = 1,500

Circle the correct products for these decimal multiplication problems.

1. 2.5 x 1,000 = 25,000 or 2,500

2. 52 x 1,000 = 52,000 or 5,200

3. 56.7 x 1,000 = 56,700 or 5,670

4. 99.3 x 1,000 = 99,300 or 9,300

Try these yourself.

1. 100.4 x 1,000 = ______

2. 125.9 x 1,000 = ______

3. 340.75 x 1,000 = ______

4. 503.68 x 1,000 = ______

5. 1,709.02 x 1,000 = ______

We can check your answer to the last problem.

Step 1: Find the nearest whole number to the decimal. The nearest whole number to 1,709.02 is 1,709.

Step 2: Multiply 1,709 by 1,000. You can do this calculation in your head by adding 3 zeros to the end of the number. The answer is 1,709,000. Therefore, a reasonable answer to the last multiplication will be close to this number.

Divide Decimals by Powers of Ten

Deleting zeros at the end of the number doesn't work when we divide decimals. We need to move the decimal point to the left to decrease the value of the number.

✗ 4.20 ÷ 10 = 4.2 is wrong because the number is still the same value

✔ 4.20 ÷ 10 = 0.42 is correct because 0.42 is 10 times less than 4.20

The arrows below show you the decimal moves one place to the left when we divide by 10 and two places to the left when we divide by 100.

15.0 ÷ 10 = 1.50

1 5 . 0

Or we can write 1.5

15.0 ÷ 100 = 0.15

1 5 . 0

We write 0.15 with zero as a placeholder

Circle the correct quotients for these decimal division problems.

1. 2.5 ÷ 10 = 0.25 or 25
2. 17.3 ÷ 10 = 173 or 1.73
3. 48.6 ÷ 10 = 486 or 4.86
4. 384.0 ÷ 100 = 3.84 or 38.4
5. 52.0 ÷ 100 = 5.20 or 0.52
6. 499.0 ÷ 100 = 4.99 or 49.90

If you are unsure of your answer, there is a quick way of checking. Look at the last division as an example.

Step 1: Find the nearest ten or nearest hundred. The nearest hundred is 500.

Step 2: Divide 500 by 100. The answer is 5. So a reasonable answer will be close to 5.

Step 3: Choose between 4.99 or 49.90. The answer must be 4.99!

Note for parent: This activity helps children understand that when we move a decimal point to the left we are decreasing the value of the number.

When we divide by 1,000 we move the decimal three places to the left.

When there are no more digits on the left we add zeros as placeholders.

15.0 ÷ 1,000 = 0.015

0 0 1 5 . 0

When we divide by 1,000 it is like dividing by 10 three times. The numbers are getting smaller each time we divide.

15.0 ÷ 10 = 1.5 — 1 and 5 tenths

1.5 ÷ 10 = 0.15 — 15 hundredths

0.15 ÷ 10 = 0.015 — 15 thousandths

Circle the correct quotients for these decimal division problems.

1. 70.0 ÷ 1,000 = 0.07 or 0.70
2. 150.0 ÷ 1,000 = 0.15 or 15.0
3. 540.0 ÷ 1,000 = 0.54 or 5,400
4. 5,550.0 ÷ 1,000 = 5.55 or 55.50

Try these yourself. Look for a pattern in your answers.

1. 5,000.0 ÷ 1,000 = [ ]
   5 0 0 0 . 0
2. 500.0 ÷ 1,000 = [ ]
   5 0 0 . 0
3. 50.0 ÷ 1,000 = [ ]
   5 0 . 0
4. 5.0 ÷ 1,000 = [ ]
   5 . 0

Decimal Addition

Decimal addition is just like whole number addition but you need to make sure you line up the decimal points and digits in the correct columns.

H	T	U		Ths	Hths
		1		1	
	6	3	.	2	5
+	3	5	.	8	7
	9	9	.	1	2

Tens	Units		Tenths	Hundredths
6	3	.	2	5
3	5	.	8	7

Carry over 1 tenth.

Carry over 1 unit.

12.50 = $12\frac{5}{10}$ or $12\frac{50}{100}$ **12.05** = $12\frac{5}{100}$

H	T	U		Ths	Hths
	1	2	.	5	0
+	1	2	.	0	5
			.		

Tens	Units		Tenths	Hundredths
1	2	.	5	0
1	2	.	0	5

Notice the importance of 0 as a placeholder in the two decimal numbers.

Copy the decimal numbers into the columns then complete the sums.

487.19 + 27.82

	H T U		Ths Hths
		.	
+		.	
		.	

362.37 + 56.90

	H T U		Ths Hths
		.	
+		.	
		.	

518.38 + 291.29

	H T U		Ths Hths
		.	
+		.	
		.	

Note for parent: This activity reminds children of the importance of 0 as a placeholder in decimal numbers and what it means.

Decimal Subtraction

Decimal subtraction is just like whole number subtraction but you need to make sure you line up the decimal points and digits in the correct columns.

75.26 — 42.17

H T U Ths Hths

1 16

7 5 . 2 6

− 4 2 . 1 7

3 3 . 0 9

Exchange 1 tenth to 10 hundredths.

Tens	Units		Tenths	Hundredths
7	5	.	2	6
4	2	.	1	7

Check the answer using addition.

H T U Ths Hths

3 3 . 0 9

\+ 4 2 . 1 7

.

93.58 — 21.68

H T U Ths Hths

2 15

9 3 . 5 8

− 2 1 . 6 8

Exchange 1 unit to 10 tenths.

Tens	Units		Tenths	Hundredths
9	3	.	5	8
2	1	.	6	8

H T U Ths Hths

Check the answer using addition.

Decimal Multiplication

Multiplying decimals is like whole number multiplication except that when you have your product, you then have to write the decimal in the correct place.

Follow these steps:

Step 1: Multiply in the normal way, ignoring the decimals.

Step 2: Count the total number of decimal places after the decimal point in both factors.

Step 3: Go to your answer and count back from the right the total number of places, then write the decimal point.

Step 4: Check that your product is reasonable.

0.6 x 0.3 =

```
    1
  0.6   ← ┐ 2 decimal places in total
x 0.3   ← ┘
-----
   18   ← 6 x 3 = 18. Write 8 units. Carry over 1 ten. 0 x 3 = 0. Plus 1 ten.
.....
  000   ← The zero on the right is a placeholder. Then 6 x 0 = 0 and 0 x 0 = 0.
+ 018   ← Find the total.
.....
  018   ← Count back 2 places and write the decimal point.
```

Product = 0.18 We say, "18 hundredths."

This product seems reasonable because we know that 6 x 3 = 18

5.96 x 1.4 =

```
   3 2
   5.96   ← ┐ 3 decimal places in total
x   1.4   ← ┘
-------
   2384   ┐ Ignore the decimals when multiplying here.
+  5960   ┘
.......
   8344
.......
   8344   ← Count back 3 places and write the decimal point.
```

Product = 8.344

We say, "Eight and three hundred forty-four thousandths."

This product seems reasonable if we round the factors to 6 x 1.5 (or $6 \times 1\frac{1}{2}$) = 9

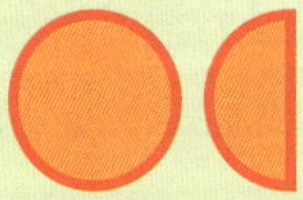

X 6 = 1.5 + 1.5 + 1.5 + 1.5 + 1.5 + 1.5 = 9 (each pair of 1.5 + 1.5 joined by an arrow labelled 3)

Note for parent: You can help your child to think of different ways to check the products by rounding and/or visualizing the factors.

Here are some more decimal multiplication problems.

8.96 x 4 =

```
  8.9 6   ← 2 decimal places
x     4   ← 4 is a whole number so multiply as you would normally do.
________

........
```

Product = [ ]

Round the 8.96 to a whole factor to check if your product is reasonable.

1.01 x 0.5 =

```
  1.0 1  ┐
x   0.5  ┘ 3 decimal places in total
________

+
........

........
```

If you round the factors, this is like 1 x 0.5 (or 0.5 x 1) = 0.5 so your product will be close to 0.5

Product = [ ]

6.95 x 5.1 =

```
  6.9 5
x   5.1
________

+
........

........
```

Round the factors to check if your product is reasonable.

Product = [ ]

17.45 x 3.2 =

```
  1 7.4 5
x     3.2
__________

+
........

........
```

Product = [ ]

Dividing Decimals

If your divisor is a whole number, dividing decimals is like whole number division. All you have to do is to write the decimal in your quotient directly above the decimal in the dividend.

Follow these steps:

Step 1: Check the divisor. If this is a whole number, write the decimal on the answer line directly above the decimal in the dividend.

Step 2: Divide in the usual way.

Step 3: Check that your quotient is reasonable.

Remember the terms:

```
         quotient
divisor | dividend
```

97.5 ÷ 3 =

Long division:

```
   32.5
3 | 97.5
  − 9
    07
  −  6
     15
  −  15
      0
```

Write the decimal on the answer line directly above.

Short division:

```
   32.5
3 | 97.¹5
```

We say, "Thirty-two and five tenths." This quotient seems reasonable because 90 ÷ 3 = 30

30	30	30

Try these using short division.

36.6 ÷ 6 =

6 | 36.6

28.44 ÷ 4 =

4 | 28.44

837.6 ÷ 2 =

2 | 837.6

Note for parent: Children can apply different strategies to solve these division problems. This activity uses written methods combined with reasoning skills and modeling.

If your divisor is a decimal number then you will need to make it a whole number by moving the decimal point. Then whatever you do to the divisor you do to the dividend.

Follow these steps:

Step 1: Multiply the decimal divisor by a power of 10 to make a whole number, and move the decimal point to the right.

Step 2: Whatever you do to the divisor, you have to do the same to the dividend.

Step 3: Divide in the usual way.

Step 4: Check that your quotient is reasonable.

$$14.4 \div 1.2 = 14.4 \div 1.2 = 144 \div 12$$

(14.4 × 10; 1.2 × 10)

$$\begin{array}{r} 12. \\ 12\,\overline{)\,144.} \\ -\ 12 \\ \hline 24 \\ -\ 24 \\ \hline 0 \end{array}$$

How many groups of 12 are in 144? You can do this division mentally if you know your times tables.

Try these using short division.

$98.8 \div 0.4 =$

$98.8 \div 0.4$

(× 10; × 10)

$= 988 \div 4$

[ ]

$4\,\overline{)\,988.}$

Check that your quotient is reasonable. Remember 1,000 ÷ 4 = 250. Is your answer close to this?

$25.5 \div 0.5 =$

$25.5 \div 0.5$

(× 10; × 10)

$= 255 \div 5$

[ ]

$5\,\overline{)\,255.}$

Order of Operations

An operation in math can be addition, subtraction, multiplication, division, or rounding, etc. When a math calculation includes different operations, we need to know the order in which we solve the operations. The order of operations is called the PEMDAS rule.

P — Parentheses	**Step 1:** All operations inside parentheses are solved first.
E — Exponent	**Step 2:** All exponential operations come second in priority.
M — Multiplication **D** — Division	**Step 3:** Solve these in order from left to right.
A — Addition **S** — Subtraction	**Step 4:** Solve these in order from left to right.

Look at this example:

$(8 + 4) \times 3 - 6 =$

$12 \times 3 - 6 =$

$36 - 6 =$

30

Follow the PEMDAS rule to solve these:

1. $(10 + 5) \times 2 - 20 =$

   $\square \times 2 - 20 =$

   $\square - 20 =$

   $\square$

2. $24 \div (12 - 6) =$

   $24 \div \square =$

   $\square$

3. $5^2 - 15 + 4 =$

   $\square - 15 + 4 =$

   $\square + 4 =$

   $\square$

4. $(24 + 4) \div 7 -$

   $\square \div 7 =$

   $\square$

Note for parent: Remind children that 5^2 is 5 x 5 not 5 x 2. This activity is preparation for algebraic thinking.

Try to solve these calculations.

5. $(7 - 3)^2 - 12 \div 2 + 5 \times 2$

....

....

....

....

7. $6^2 + (9 - 3) + 18 \div 9$

....

....

....

....

6. $5 \times (8 + 4) + 14 \div 2$

....

....

....

....

8. $10^2 + (25 \div 5) - 50 \div 5$

....

....

....

....

The order in which we carry out operations is important so we all arrive at the same answer. What happens if there are no parentheses or exponents in a math expression?

Which of these is correct? $1 + 2 \times 3 = 9$ or $1 + 2 \times 3 = 7$
When there are no parentheses or exponents we go to the third step.

We multiply before adding, so the correct answer is 7.

Circle the correct answers below.

1. $18 - 4 \times 2 = 28$ or $18 - 4 \times 2 = 10$
2. $10 + 5 \times 3 = 25$ or $10 + 5 \times 3 = 45$
3. $12 - 9 \div 3 + 6 = 15$ or $12 - 9 \div 3 + 6 = 7$

Remember, we multiply and/or divide (from left to right in order) before we add and/or subtract.

Graphing Number Patterns

Write the **x** and **y** numbers from the table as coordinates in the column on the right.

x	y	Coordinates
1	1	(1, 1)
2	2	(2, 2)
3	3	
4	4	
5	5	
6	6	

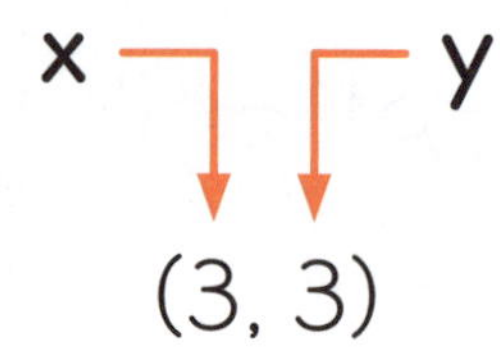

The **x** number is separated from the **y** number with a comma, and parentheses are drawn around them.

Look at the grid below. It is made up of two perpendicular number lines. The point where the lines cross is labeled 0 on each line. This is the "origin."

The horizontal line going across is the **x** axis and the vertical line going up is the **y** axis.

To plot (1, 1) on the grid, start on the **x** axis at 1 then go up the **y** axis to reach 1.

Mark the place where the lines meet with a dot.

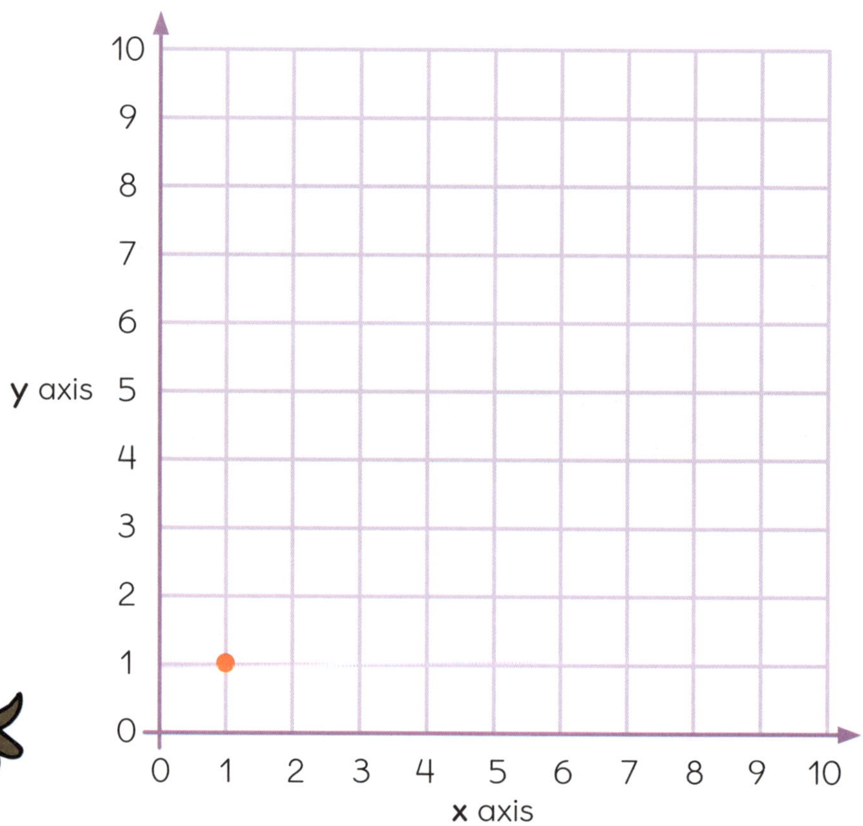

Now plot the remaining coordinates on the grid.

Note for parent: The x axis always goes across the bottom of the grid. You can remember this by thinking of "across" as "a cross"—in other words an x!

Complete the columns for **x** and **y**, and the coordinates column, then plot the coordinates on the grid.

x	y	Coordinates
0	9	(0, 9)
1	8	
2	7	
3		
	5	
5	4	

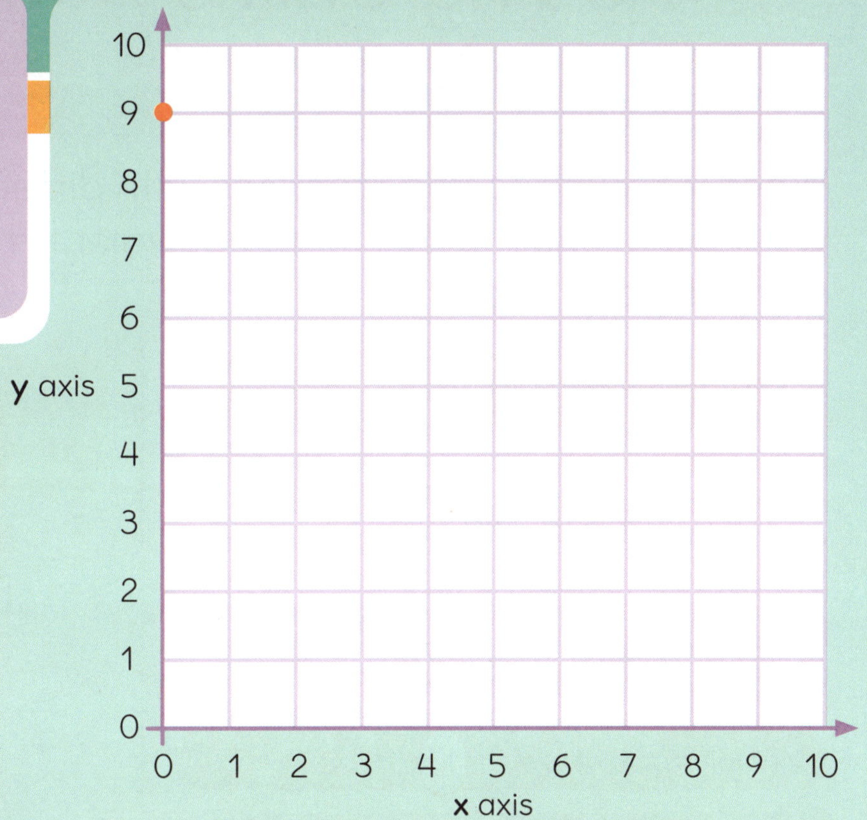

x	y	Coordinates
0	5	(0, 5)
1	5	
2	5	
	5	
4	5	
	5	

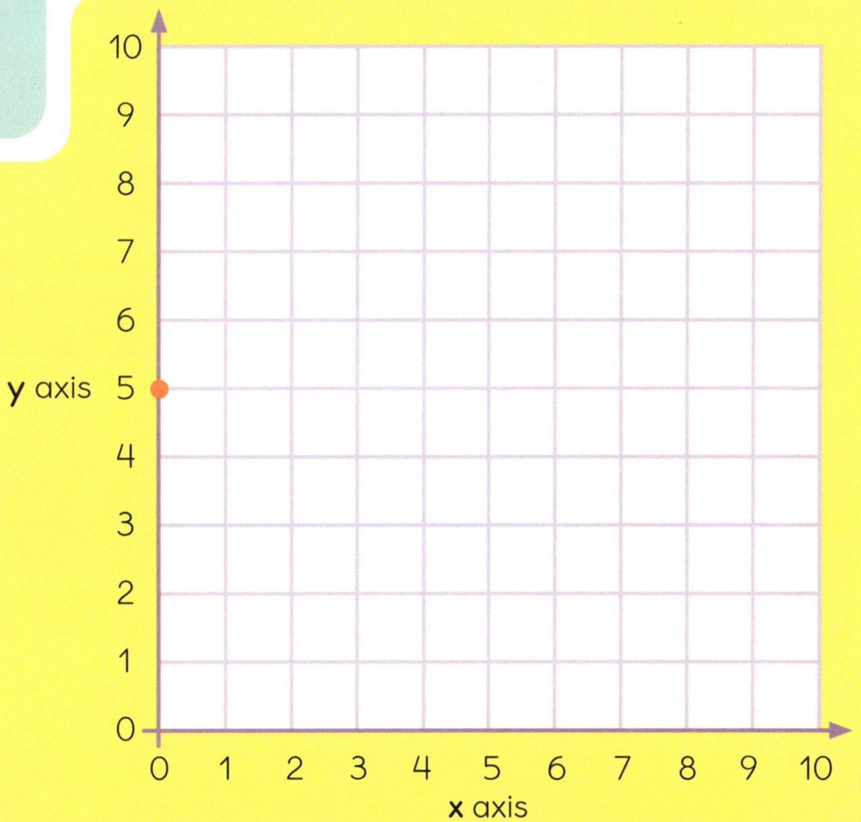

Adding Unlike Denominators

When we want to add fractions with different denominators, we have to change them into equivalent fractions with the same denominator.

Step 1: Find the least common multiple.

$$\frac{2}{3} + \frac{3}{4}$$

Multiples of 3 are: 3, 6, 9, 12, 15...

Multiples of 4 are: 4, 8, 12, 16...

12 is the least common multiple of 3 and 4.

Step 2: Change to equivalent fractions with 12 as the denominator.

$$\frac{2}{3} = \frac{8}{12} \quad (\times 4) \qquad \text{and} \qquad \frac{3}{4} = \frac{9}{12} \quad (\times 3)$$

Step 3: Add the numerators.

$$\frac{8}{12} + \frac{9}{12} = \frac{17}{12}$$

Step 4: Convert to a mixed number if needed.

$$\frac{17}{12} = 1\frac{5}{12}$$

Figure these out for yourself.

$$\frac{5}{6} + \frac{3}{4}$$

$$2\frac{3}{5} + 1\frac{3}{10}$$

With mixed numbers, add the fractions part first then the whole numbers.

Note for parent: When comparing two unlike denominators, it is a good idea to write down the multiples in order to find the least common multiple.

Try these yourself. Change to equivalent fractions with the same denominator. Simplify your answers to lowest terms. Use the space for your work. The first one is done for you.

1. $\frac{1}{4} + \frac{1}{8} = \frac{2}{8} + \frac{1}{8} = \frac{3}{8}$

2. $1\frac{1}{3} + 2\frac{1}{9} =$

3. $2\frac{1}{3} + 2\frac{1}{4} =$

4. $\frac{1}{4} + \frac{1}{12} =$

5. $\frac{3}{5} + \frac{1}{15} =$

6. $\frac{2}{3} + \frac{1}{6} =$

Subtracting Unlike Denominators

Just like with addition, to subtract fractions with different denominators, you need to find the least common multiple and give the fractions the same denominator.

Step 1:
Find the least common multiple.

$$\frac{5}{6} - \frac{1}{4}$$

Multiples of 6 are: 6, 12, 18...

Multiples of 4 are: 4, 8, 12, 16...

12 is the least common multiple of 6 and 4.

Step 2:
Change to equivalent fractions with 12 as the denominator.

$$\frac{5 \times 2}{6 \times 2} = \frac{10}{12} \qquad \frac{1 \times 3}{4 \times 3} = \frac{3}{12}$$

Step 3:
Subtract the numerators.

$$\frac{10}{12} - \frac{3}{12} = \frac{7}{12}$$

Step 4:
Convert to a mixed number or simplify if needed.

$$\frac{7}{12}$$

This fraction can't be converted to a mixed number or simplified so this is our answer.

Note for parent: With mixed numbers, subtract the fraction part first then the whole numbers.

Try these yourself. Change to equivalent fractions with the same denominator. Use the space for your work.

1. $\frac{3}{4} - \frac{1}{8} = \square$

2. $\frac{10}{12} - \frac{3}{4} = \square$

3. $\frac{1}{3} - \frac{1}{4} = \square$

4. $\frac{7}{8} - \frac{3}{4} = \square$

5. $5\frac{3}{4} - 2\frac{1}{8} = \square\ \square$

6. $5\frac{4}{5} - 2\frac{3}{12} = \square\ \square$

7. $7\frac{7}{8} - 3\frac{1}{4} = \square\ \square$

8. $6\frac{1}{2} - 4\frac{3}{8} = \square\ \square$

Adding Tenths and Hundredths

We can add tenths and hundredths together if we give them the same denominator.

$$\frac{3}{10} + \frac{4}{100} = \frac{30}{100} + \frac{4}{100} = \frac{34}{100} = \frac{17}{50}$$

(x10 on the numerator and the denominator; + on the numerators)

Try these yourself. First, change the tenths to hundredths. Then add the numerators, and simplify to lowest terms.

(x10, x10, +)

$$\frac{2}{10} + \frac{2}{100} = \frac{\square}{100} + \frac{2}{100} = \frac{\square}{100} = \boxed{\frac{\quad}{\quad}}$$

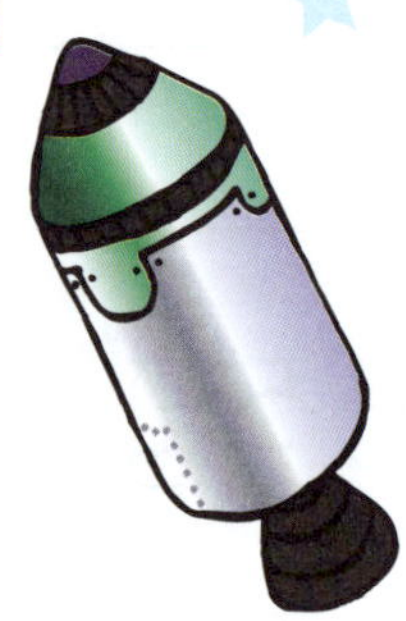

(x10, x10, +)

$$\frac{4}{10} + \frac{5}{100} = \frac{\square}{100} + \frac{5}{100} = \frac{\square}{100} = \boxed{\frac{\quad}{\quad}}$$

Note for parent: Adding tenths and hundredths is introduced briefly in fourth grade, with further practice in fifth grade.

Subtracting Tenths and Hundredths

We can subtract tenths and hundredths if we give them the same denominator.

$$\frac{6}{10} - \frac{5}{100} = \frac{60}{100} - \frac{5}{100} = \frac{55}{100} = \frac{11}{20}$$

Figure these out yourself. First, change tenths to hundredths. Then subtract the numerators, and simplify to lowest terms. Use the space for your work.

$$\frac{75}{100} - \frac{7}{10} = \square$$

$$\frac{5}{10} - \frac{20}{100} = \square$$

$$\frac{40}{100} - \frac{3}{10} = \square$$

Note for parent: We multiply by 10 to change tenths to hundredths. One tenth is 10 times greater than one hundredth.

Word Problems Using Equivalents

Rewrite these word problems as equivalent fractions and add or subtract to find the answers. Use the models to help.

1. $\frac{1}{3}$ of the cookies in a jar are chocolate, $\frac{1}{4}$ are ginger, and the rest are caramel. What fraction is caramel-flavored?

To make the math easier, we need to change these fractions to equivalents.

$\frac{1}{3} = \frac{\square}{12}$ $\quad$ $\frac{1}{4} = \frac{\square}{12}$

Now we can draw a model divided into 12 sections.

$\frac{\square}{12} + \frac{\square}{12} = \frac{\square}{12}$

$\frac{12}{12} - \frac{\square}{12} = \frac{\square}{12}$

$\frac{\square}{12}$ are caramel-flavored.

2. Lizzie uses $\frac{3}{5}$ of a bag of flour to make pizza dough and $\frac{1}{3}$ to make a pie crust. What fraction of the flour is left?

Change the fractions to equivalents and use the model.

$\frac{3}{5} = \frac{\square}{15}$ $\quad$ $\frac{1}{3} = \frac{\square}{15}$

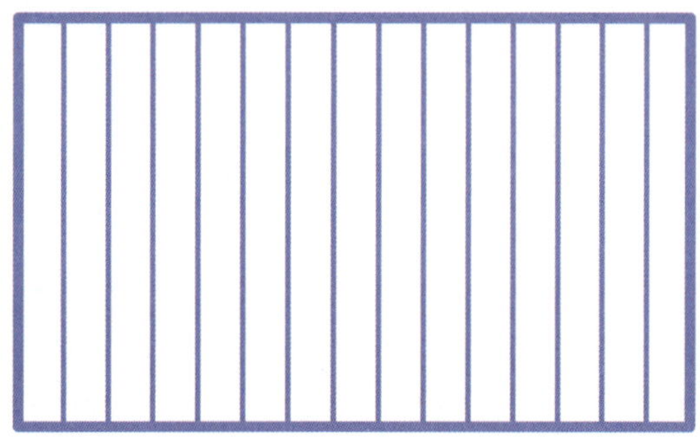

$\frac{\square}{15} + \frac{\square}{15} = \frac{\square}{15}$

$\frac{15}{15} - \frac{\square}{15} = \frac{\square}{15}$

$\frac{\square}{15}$ of the flour is left.

Note for parent: Children can draw models or use equations to solve these problems. Encourage them to check that their answers are correct.

3. Franklin learned $\frac{2}{3}$ of the Spanish words on the spelling list and Walter learned $\frac{4}{5}$. Who learned more words and by what fraction?

Change the fractions to equivalents and use the model.

$\frac{2}{3} = \frac{\square}{15}$ $\frac{4}{5} = \frac{\square}{15}$

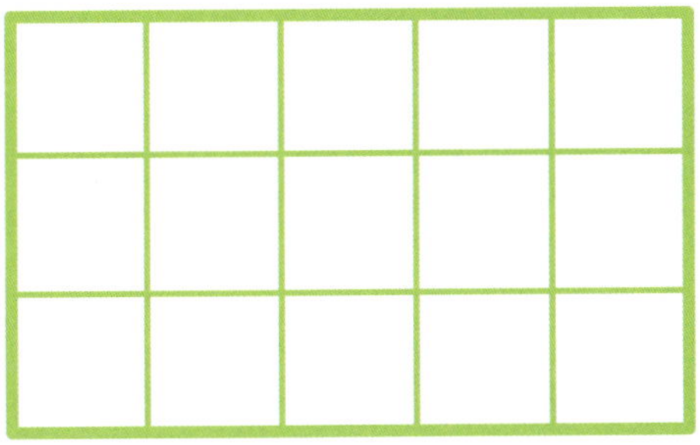

$\frac{\square}{15} - \frac{\square}{15} = \frac{\square}{15}$

.... learned

$\frac{\square}{15}$ more words.

4. Nina completed $\frac{3}{4}$ of her homework yesterday and $\frac{1}{6}$ today. What fraction of her homework did she complete? What fraction is left?

Change the fractions to equivalents and use the model.

$\frac{3}{4} = \frac{\square}{12}$ $\frac{1}{6} = \frac{\square}{12}$

$\frac{\square}{12} + \frac{\square}{12} = \frac{\square}{12}$

$\frac{12}{12} - \frac{\square}{12} = \frac{\square}{12}$

$\frac{\square}{12}$ of Nina's homework still needs to be completed.

Fractions and Division

Fractions and division are related. The fraction $\frac{1}{2}$ means 1 whole divided by 2.

We can write: $\frac{1}{2}$ or $1 \div 2$ or $2\overline{)1}$

Rewrite these word problems as fractions and divide to find the answers or quotients.

Example: Three friends wash their neighbors' cars. They earn 36 dollars in total which they share equally. Write a fraction that shows how much money they each earn.

We can write this as: $36 \div 3$ or $3\overline{)36}$

or as a fraction: $\frac{36}{3}$

36 ← Total money they earn

3 ← Shared by 3 friends

$\frac{36}{3} = \square$ They each earn $\square$ dollars.

Remember the terms :

numerator and dividend → 20

denominator and divisor → 5

$\frac{20}{5} = 4$ ← answer or quotient

Try these yourself.

1. Alex has 24 party favors that he wants to share equally into 6 party bags. How many party favors go into each bag?

$\frac{\square}{6} = \square$ party favors in each bag.

2. Amir is planting flower bulbs. He has 64 bulbs in total and 8 plant pots. If he divides the bulbs equally between the pots, how many bulbs go in each pot?

$\frac{64}{\square} = \square$ bulbs in each pot.

Note for parent: This activity demonstrates how fractions and division (which is often called "sharing" in word problems) are related.

If there is a remainder in the quotient, you can convert this to a fraction.

$$\frac{7}{2} = 3 \text{ r } 1 = 3\frac{1}{2}$$ ← The remainder is $\frac{1}{2}$ because this is 1 ÷ 2.

$$\frac{37}{6} = 6 \text{ r } 1 = 6\frac{1}{6}$$ ← The remainder is $\frac{1}{6}$ because this is 1 ÷ 6.

Try these. They have remainders that you need to convert to fractions.

3. Ruby and Reggie are together writing a 19-page drama script. If they share the writing, how many pages do they each have to write?

They each have to write $\frac{19}{\square} = \square \frac{\square}{\square}$ pages.

4. A teacher has 28 sheets of colored paper that she wants to share equally with 8 children. How many sheets of colored paper do they each get?

They each get $\frac{\square}{8} = \square \frac{\square}{\square} = \square \frac{\square}{\square}$ sheets.

Multiply a Fraction by a Whole Number

Multiplying a fraction by a whole number is like repeated addition.

$6 \times \frac{1}{2} =$ 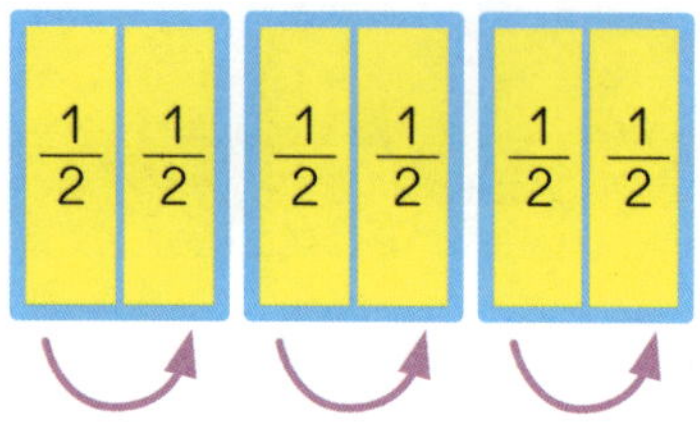

$= \frac{1}{2} + \frac{1}{2} + \frac{1}{2} + \frac{1}{2} + \frac{1}{2} + \frac{1}{2} = \frac{6}{2} = 3$

1 + 1 + 1 ← Count the whole numbers.

Try these. Write your answers in the simplest form. You can color the models to help you.

1. $5 \times \frac{1}{3} =$ [ ][ ] $= \frac{\square}{\square} = \square\frac{\square}{\square}$

2. $7 \times \frac{1}{4} =$ [ ][ ] $= \frac{\square}{\square} = \square\frac{\square}{\square}$

3. $6 \times \frac{1}{5} =$ [ ][ ] $= \frac{\square}{\square} = \square\frac{\square}{\square}$

4. $7 \times \frac{1}{6} =$ [ ][ ] $= \frac{\square}{\square} = \square\frac{\square}{\square}$

Note for parent: Children need to be familiar with different strategies for problem solving. With simple fractions, visual models work well, and children can draw these for themselves.

Look at this example:

$3 \times \frac{2}{5} =$

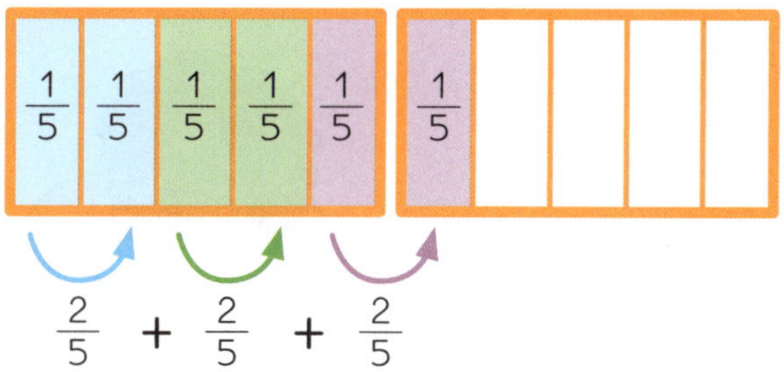

$= \frac{2}{5} + \frac{2}{5} + \frac{2}{5} = \frac{6}{5} = 1\frac{1}{5}$

This improper fraction becomes a mixed number.

Try these. Write your answers in the simplest form.
You can color the models to help you.

1. $4 \times \frac{2}{3} =$ ☐☐☐ ☐☐☐ ☐☐☐ $= \frac{\square}{\square} = \square\frac{\square}{\square}$

2. $2 \times \frac{3}{4} =$ ☐☐☐☐ ☐☐☐☐ $= \frac{\square}{\square} = \square\frac{\square}{\square}$

3. $5 \times \frac{2}{5} =$ ☐☐☐☐☐ ☐☐☐☐☐ $= \frac{\square}{\square} = \square$

4. $3 \times \frac{2}{3} =$ ☐☐☐ ☐☐☐ $= \frac{\square}{\square} = \square$

Multiply the Quick Way

Here is a quicker method you can use to multiply fractions. For example:

	Step 1		Step 2		Step 3
$3 \times \frac{2}{3} =$	$\frac{3}{1}$	$\times$	$\frac{2}{3}$	$=$	$\frac{6}{3} = 2$

Step 1:
Take the first factor (the whole number) and turn it into a fraction with 3 as the numerator and 1 as the denominator.

Step 2:
Multiply the numerator by the numerator, and the denominator by the denominator.

Step 3:
Simplify the fraction if you can.

Notice our product (which is the answer 2) is less than the first factor we started with (3) because we multiplied by another factor that was less than 1 (it was $\frac{2}{3}$).

Try these yourself.

1. $4 \times \frac{3}{5} = \frac{\square}{1} \times \frac{3}{5} = \frac{\square}{\square} = \square\,\frac{\square}{\square}$

Write the whole number as a fraction with 1 as the denominator.

Note for parent: Remember, a whole number always has 1 as its denominator.

2. $5 \times \frac{5}{6} = \frac{\square}{1} \times \frac{5}{6} = \frac{\square}{\square} = \square\frac{\square}{\square}$

3. $3 \times \frac{3}{4} = \frac{\square}{1} \times \frac{3}{4} = \frac{\square}{\square} = \square\frac{\square}{\square}$

4. $6 \times \frac{5}{8} = \frac{\square}{1} \times \frac{5}{8} = \frac{\square}{\square} = \square\frac{\square}{\square} = \square\frac{\square}{\square}$

5. $7 \times \frac{3}{10} = \frac{\square}{1} \times \frac{3}{10} = \frac{\square}{\square} = \square\frac{\square}{\square}$

6. $8 \times \frac{7}{8} = \frac{\square}{1} \times \frac{7}{8} = \frac{\square}{\square} = \square$

7. $9 \times \frac{5}{12} = \frac{\square}{1} \times \frac{5}{12} = \frac{\square}{\square} = \square\frac{\square}{\square} = \square\frac{\square}{\square}$

Multiply a Fraction by a Fraction

If I have $\frac{1}{2}$ a candy bar and my 2 friends share it with me, we each have $\frac{1}{3}$ of $\frac{1}{2}$. How much is that?

We can solve this problem by using a model.

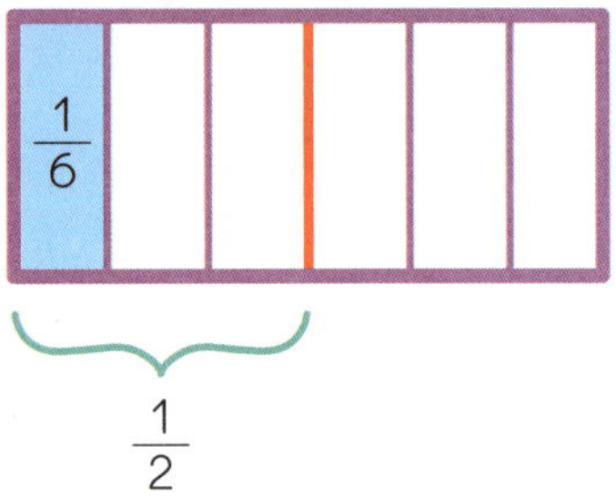

$$\frac{1}{3} \text{ of } \frac{1}{2} = \frac{1}{6}$$

Or we can write an equation:

$$\frac{1}{3} \times \frac{1}{2}$$

Read the multiplication sign as "of."

When multiplying a fraction by a fraction there is only one rule to remember: work straight across.

Multiply

$$\frac{1}{3} \times \frac{1}{2} = \frac{1}{6}$$

Check the math! Our equation and our model both give us the same answer.

Use the model and write an equation to solve these problems.

1. A puppy ate $\frac{1}{3}$ of $\frac{1}{4}$ of a bowl of dog food. How much did the puppy eat?

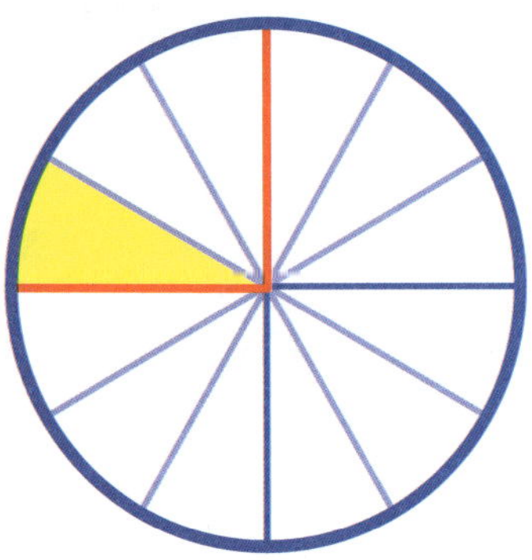

$$\frac{1}{3} \times \frac{1}{4} = \boxed{\frac{\quad}{\quad}}$$

Note for parent: Being able to draw models to represent problems is a valuable math skill. Children can then use these models to check written methods.

2. Jorge cut some banana bread into fourths and he ate $\frac{1}{2}$ of $\frac{1}{4}$. How much did he eat?

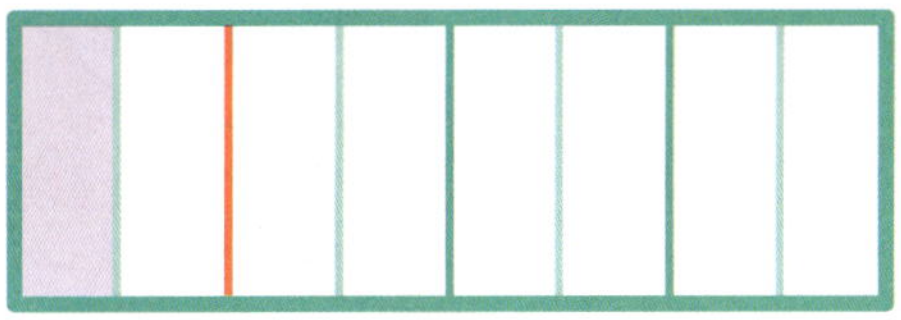

$$\frac{1}{2} \times \frac{1}{4} = \frac{\quad}{\quad}$$

3. A rabbit ate $\frac{2}{3}$ of $\frac{1}{4}$ of a carrot. How much is that?

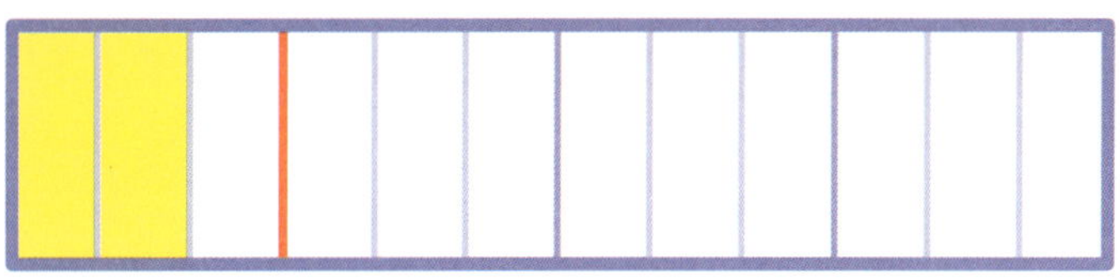

$$\frac{2}{3} \times \frac{1}{4} = \frac{\quad}{\quad} = \frac{\quad}{\quad}$$

4. I spent $\frac{3}{5}$ of $\frac{1}{2}$ of my allowance. How much is that?

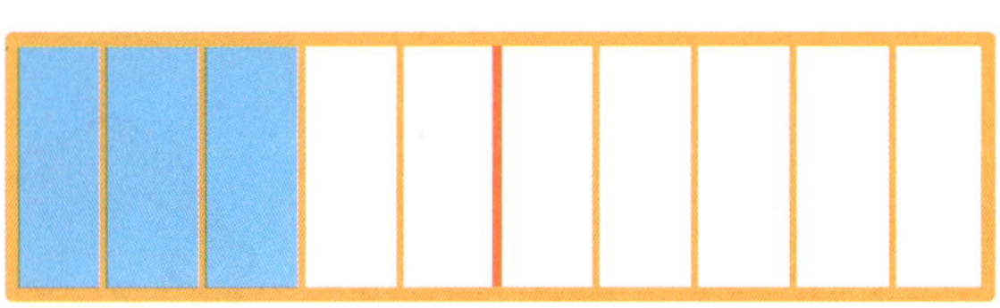

$$\frac{3}{5} \times \frac{1}{2} = \frac{\quad}{\quad}$$

Area Model Problem

We can use area models to help us solve real-life problems.

Ana has a candy bar divided into 12 sections. She eats $\frac{1}{3}$ herself and her brother Alan eats $\frac{3}{4}$ of the $\frac{2}{3}$ that is left. What fraction of the total candy bar does Alan eat?

We can draw this problem as an area model.

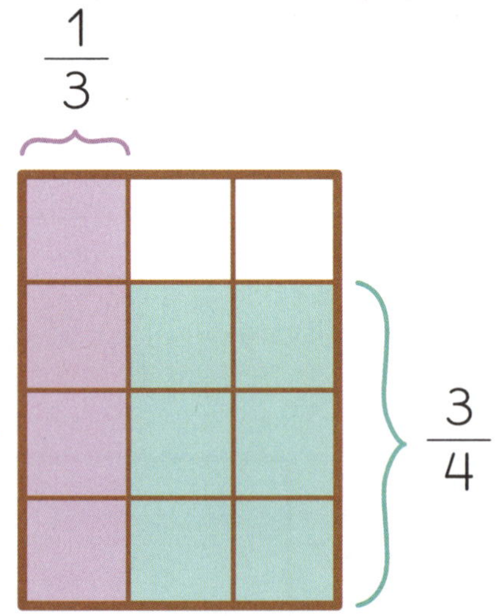

Step 1: Draw a rectangle and divide it into 12 equal sections.

Step 2: Color $\frac{1}{3}$ to represent what Ana eats.

Step 3: Color $\frac{3}{4}$ to represent what Alan eats.

Step 4: Count the sections eaten by Alan. → Alan eats ☐ sections.

Step 5: Write what Alan eats as a fraction of the total candy bar.

Number of sections Alan eats:
Total number of sections in the candy bar:

$\frac{\square}{\square} = \frac{\square}{\square}$

Step 6: Check the math.

Alan eats $\frac{3}{4} \times \frac{2}{3} = \frac{\square}{\square} = \frac{\square}{\square}$

Note for parent: Area models are a useful way to visualize fraction problems and check the accuracy of written methods.

Comparing Factors

Let's compare factors by size. For example: $7 > 7 \times \frac{1}{2}$

7 is greater than $7 \times \frac{1}{2}$ because

$$7 \times \frac{1}{2} = \frac{1}{2} + \frac{1}{2} + \frac{1}{2} + \frac{1}{2} + \frac{1}{2} + \frac{1}{2} + \frac{1}{2} = 3\frac{1}{2}$$

7 is the multiplier

$\frac{1}{2}$ is the size of the group we are multiplying

Compare the size of each factor.
You don't need to multiply the factors, just indicate which is greater by writing the correct sign in the box.

> greater than **<** less than

If one of the factors we are multiplying is a whole number and the other factor is less than 1 (or is a fraction) then the product when multiplied will be less than the whole number.

1. $7 \; \square \; 7 \times 5$
2. $\frac{3}{3} \; \square \; 3 \times 3$
3. $3 \times \frac{6}{6} \; \square \; 6 \times 3$
4. $\frac{9}{10} \; \square \; 100 \times \frac{1}{2}$
5. $8 \; \square \; 8 \times \frac{1}{2}$
6. $5 \times \frac{1}{10} \; \square \; 5 \times \frac{1}{2}$
7. $25 \; \square \; 25 \times \frac{1}{5}$
8. $99 \times \frac{1}{4} \; \square \; 99$

Note for parent: This activity requires children to look at whole numbers and fractions (before carrying out any calculations) and think about what the numbers mean.

Multiply Fractions and Mixed Numbers

Read the problems and use the models to find the products.

1. A recipe for 4 people states that we need $2\frac{1}{2}$ cups of flour. How much flour do we need for 2 people? We need to reduce the quantity of flour by half. We can use a model to solve this problem.

$\frac{1}{2}$ of $2\frac{1}{2}$ $\qquad 1 + 1 + \frac{1}{2} = 2\frac{1}{2}$ cups for 4 people

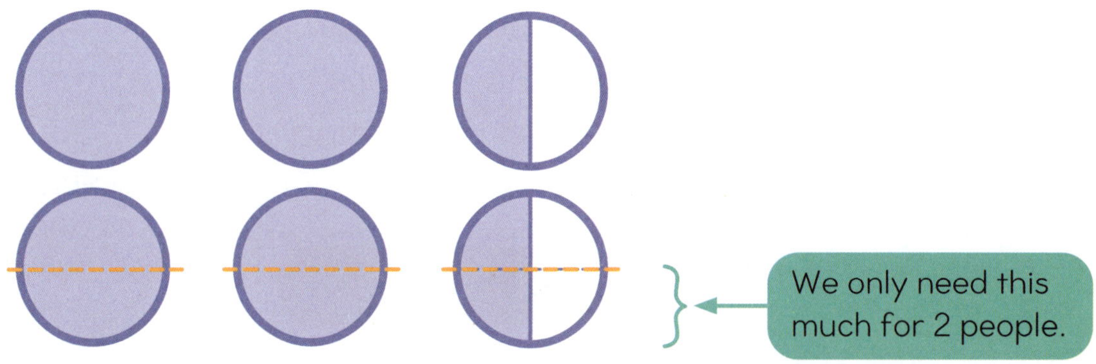

$\frac{1}{2} + \frac{1}{2} + \frac{1}{4} = 1\frac{1}{4}$ cups for 2 people

Or we can write an equation: $\frac{1}{2} \times 2\frac{1}{2} = \frac{1}{2} \times \frac{5}{2} = \frac{5}{4} = 1\frac{1}{4}$

Step 1: Convert mixed numbers to improper fractions.

5 halves

$2\frac{1}{2} = \frac{5}{2}$

There is a quick way: $2\frac{{}^{+}1}{{}_{\times}2} = \frac{5}{2}$

$2 \times 2 + 1 = 5$

Step 2: Multiply the numerators.

Step 3: Multiply the denominators.

Step 4: Simplify to lowest terms.

Step 5: Convert to a mixed number.

Note for parent: The models will help children to understand written methods.

2. If we need $2\frac{3}{4}$ cups of cocoa for 4 people, how much cocoa do we need for 2 people? Use the model to help you solve the problem.

$\frac{1}{2}$ of $2\frac{3}{4}$

$1 + 1 + \frac{3}{4} = \square\frac{\square}{\square}$ cups for 4 people

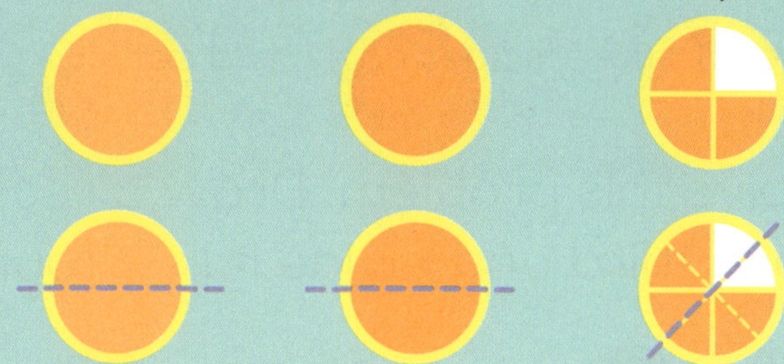

$\frac{\square}{\square} + \frac{\square}{\square} + \frac{\square}{\square} = \square\frac{\square}{\square}$ cups for 2 people

Follow the steps on the opposite page to complete the equation:

$\frac{1}{2} \times 2\frac{3}{4} = \frac{1}{2} \times \frac{\square}{\square} = \frac{\square}{\square} = \square\frac{\square}{\square}$

3. If we need $1\frac{1}{3}$ cups of sugar for 3 people, how much sugar do we need for 1 person? Use the model to help you solve the problem.

$\frac{1}{3}$ of $1\frac{1}{3}$

$1 + \frac{1}{3} = \square\frac{\square}{\square}$ cups for 3 people

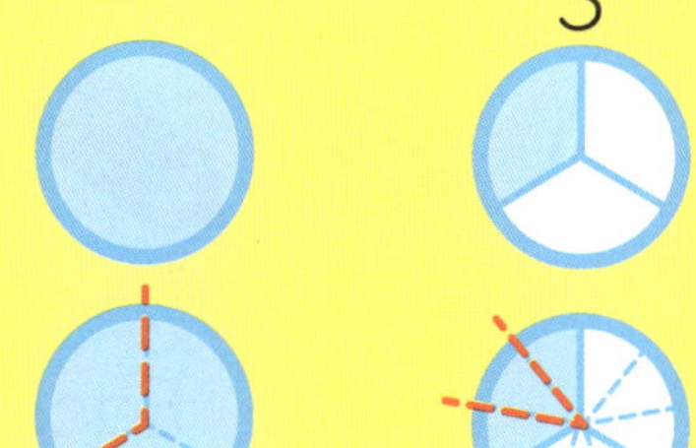

$\frac{\square}{\square} + \frac{\square}{\square} = \frac{\square}{\square}$ cup for 1 person

Follow the steps on the opposite page to complete the equation:

$\frac{1}{3} \times 1\frac{1}{3} = \frac{1}{3} \times \frac{\square}{\square} = \frac{\square}{\square}$

Divide a Fraction by a Whole Number

Read the problems and use the models to find the quotients.

1. A teacher shares $\frac{1}{3}$ of a sheet of stickers equally among 4 children. What fraction of the whole sheet of stickers does each child get?

$$\frac{1}{3} \div 4$$

We can use a model to solve this problem. Draw a rectangle and divide it into thirds. Then take one third and divide it into four sections.

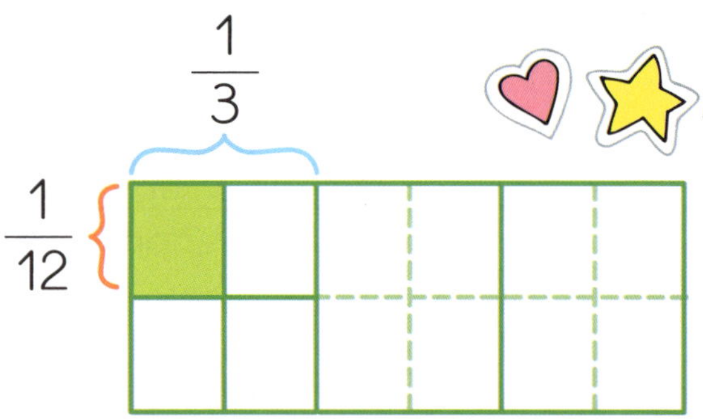

$$\frac{1}{3} \div 4 = \frac{1}{12}$$

Each child gets $\frac{\square}{\square}$ of the whole sheet of stickers.

Now we can check the quotient using multiplication because division and multiplication are inverse, or opposite, operations.

$$\frac{\square}{\square} \times 4 = \frac{1}{3}$$

2. A teacher shares $\frac{1}{2}$ of a box of pencils equally among 3 children. What fraction of all the pencils in the box does each child get?

$$\frac{1}{2} \div 3$$

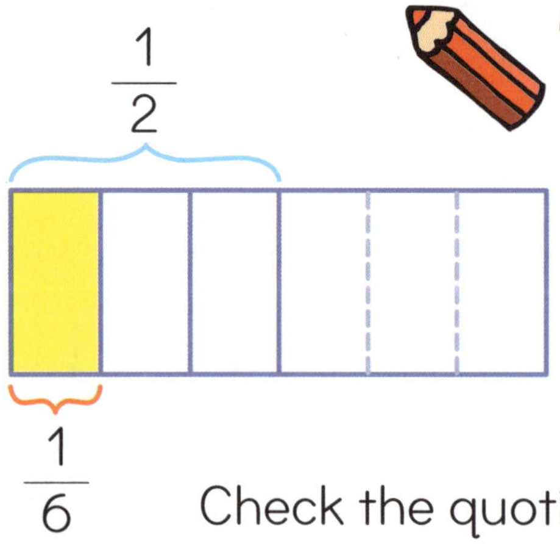

$$\frac{1}{2} \div 3 = \frac{\square}{\square}$$

Each child gets $\frac{\square}{\square}$ of the pencils in the box.

Check the quotient using multiplication: $\frac{\square}{\square} \times 3 = \frac{1}{2}$

Note for parent: Children can develop strategies to divide fractions by reasoning about the relationship between multiplication and division.

3. If I have $\frac{1}{4}$ of a pizza and I share it equally with a friend, what fraction of the whole pizza do we each get?

$$\frac{1}{4} \div 2$$

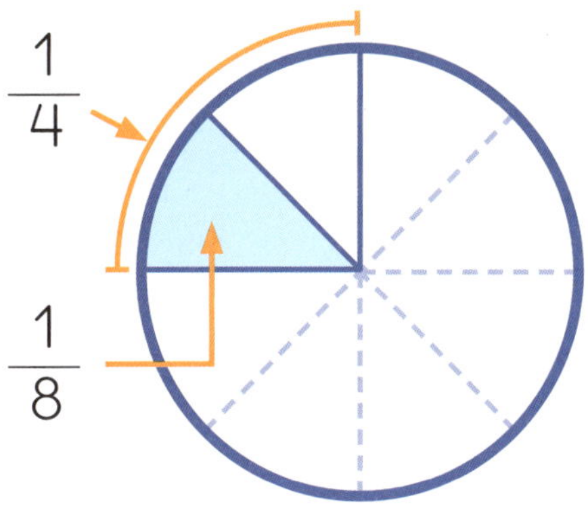

$$\frac{1}{4} \div 2 = \frac{\square}{\square}$$

We each get $\frac{\square}{\square}$ of the whole pizza.

Check the quotient using multiplication: $\frac{\square}{\square} \times 2 = \frac{\square}{\square}$

4. Jamal shares $\frac{1}{3}$ of a box of dog biscuits equally among his 3 dogs. What fraction of all the biscuits in the box does each dog get?

$$\frac{1}{3} \div 3$$

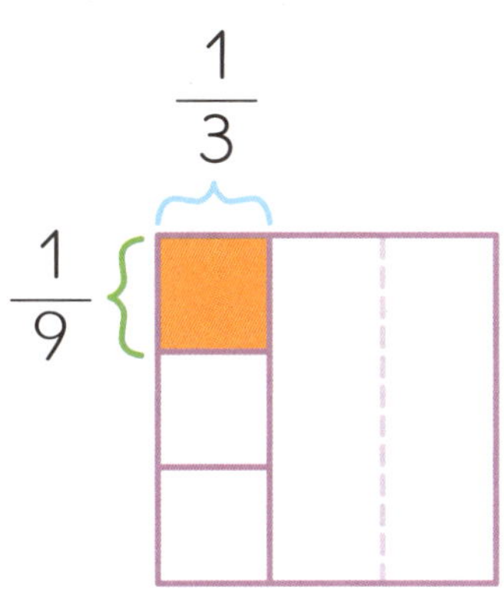

$$\frac{1}{3} \div 3 = \frac{\square}{\square}$$

Each dog gets $\frac{\square}{\square}$ of all the biscuits in the box.

Check the quotient using multiplication: $\frac{\square}{\square} \times 3 = \frac{\square}{\square}$

Divide a Whole Number by a Fraction

Read the problems and use the models to find the quotients.

1. I have 4 lengths of fabric and I cut each length into fifths. How many fifths do I have all together?

$$4 \div \frac{1}{5}$$

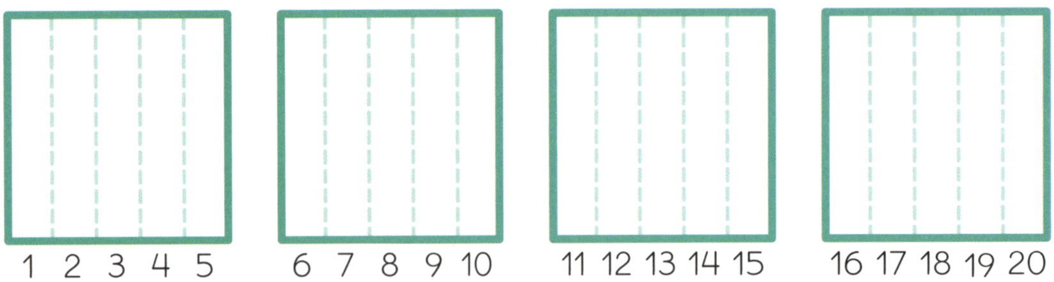

$$4 \div \frac{1}{5} = 20$$

Check the quotient using multiplication: $\square \times \frac{1}{5} = 4$

2. I have 3 circles and I cut each circle into eighths. How many eighths do I have all together?

$$3 \div \frac{1}{8}$$

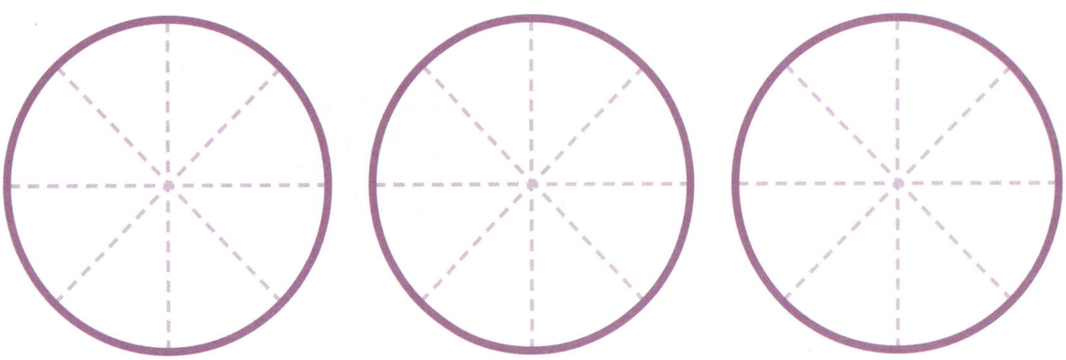

$$3 \div \frac{1}{8} = \square$$

Check the quotient using multiplication: $\square \times \frac{1}{8} = 3$

Note for parent: This activity is an introduction to the division of fractions, which is a topic that children will develop further in sixth grade.

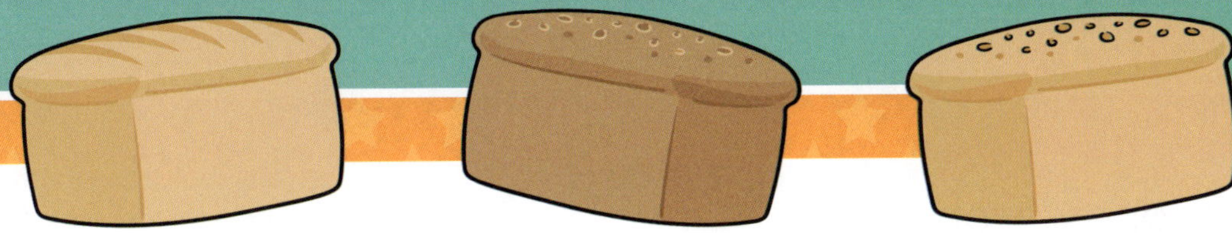

3. I have 3 loaves and I divide each loaf into sixths. How many sixths do I have all together?

$3 \div \frac{1}{6}$

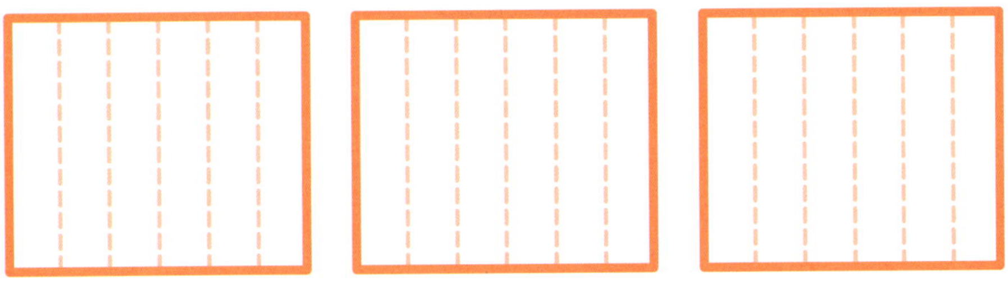

$3 \div \frac{1}{6} = \square$

Check the quotient using multiplication: $\square \times \frac{1}{6} = \square$

4. I have 4 squares and I divide each square into quarters. How many quarters do I have all together?

$4 \div \frac{1}{4}$

$4 \div \frac{1}{4} = \square$

Check the quotient using multiplication: $\square \times \frac{1}{4} = \square$

Money Problems Using Fractions

Solve the money problems.

1. What is one dollar shared among 4 friends? What fraction of one dollar does each friend get? How much is that worth in cents?

$1 \div 4 = \frac{1}{4}$ Each child gets $\frac{\square}{\square}$ of one dollar.

To find out what $\frac{1}{4}$ of one dollar is in cents, we can exchange \$1 for 100¢ then divide by 4. We can write this as a division problem or as a fraction:

$100 \div 4 = \square$ ¢ or $\frac{100}{4} = \square$ ¢ $\frac{1}{4}$ of \$1 is worth $\square$ ¢

We can check if we are correct by multiplying: $25 \times 4 = \square$

Or by drawing a model and coloring $\frac{1}{4}$ of 100.

We can write 25¢ as a fraction: $\frac{25}{100}$ or $\frac{1}{4}$

$\frac{1}{100}$

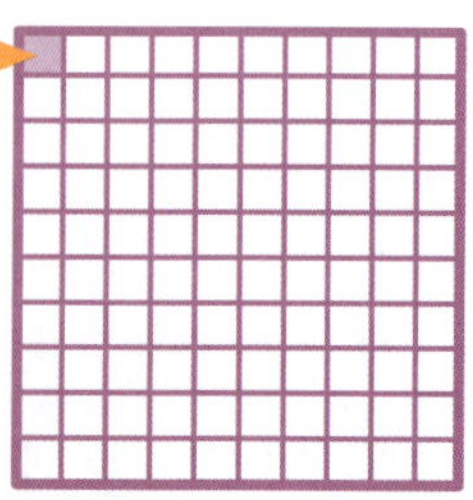

2. What is one dollar shared between 5 friends? What fraction of one dollar does each friend get? How much is that worth in cents?

$1 \div 5 = \frac{\square}{\square}$ Each child gets $\frac{\square}{\square}$ of one dollar.

First, exchange \$1 for 100¢.

$100 \div 5 = \square$ ¢ or $\frac{100}{5} = \square$ ¢ $\frac{1}{5}$ of \$1 is worth $\square$ ¢

Check if you are correct: $\square \times \square = 100$

Note for parent: Children need to practice reasoning skills that will be useful in everyday life.

3. The cashier says I owe him $\frac{3}{5}$ of a dollar. How much is that worth in cents?

If you have completed the last problem, you know that:
$\frac{1}{5}$ of a dollar = 20¢ and you can simply multiply by 3 to find $\frac{3}{5}$. So 3 x 20¢ = 60¢

Or we can do it another way.
Change fifths to hundredths: $\frac{3 \times 20}{5 \times 20} = \frac{\square}{\square}$ = 60 hundredths = $\square$ ¢

Color the model to check if you are correct.

$\frac{3}{5}$ is shaded

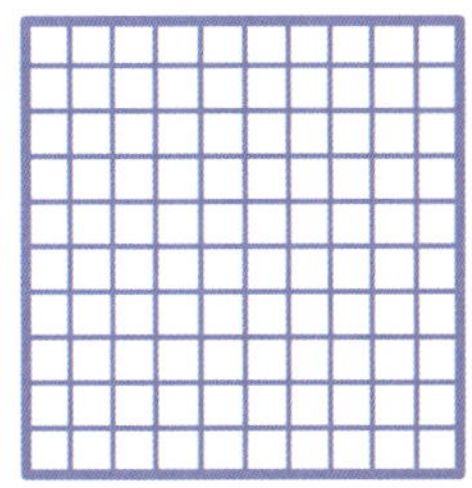

Color $\frac{60}{100}$ and compare.

4. If I have $\frac{3}{4}$ of 2 dollars, how much is that worth in cents?

If you have completed question 1, you know that:

$\frac{1}{4} = \frac{\square}{100} = \square$ ¢

Multiply by 3 to find $\frac{3}{4}$ of 1 dollar.

$\frac{3}{4} = \frac{\square}{\square} = \square$ ¢

Now multiply by 2 to find $\frac{3}{4}$ of 2 dollars.

$\square$ x 2 = $\square$ ¢

Color the model to check if you are correct.

$\frac{3}{4}$ of \$1 is shaded

Color $\frac{3}{4}$ of \$2

Money: Tenths and Hundredths

Remember: $\frac{1}{10}$ of a dollar = \$0.10 or 10¢

$\frac{1}{100}$ of a dollar = \$0.01 or 1¢

Look at this example:

$\$0.25 = \frac{2}{10} + \frac{5}{100} =$ Two tenths plus five hundredths of a dollar.

Write the value in decimal numbers.
The first one has been done for you.

1. $\frac{3}{10}$ of a dollar = \$0.30

2. Six tenths of a dollar = \$

3. $\frac{8}{10}$ plus $\frac{1}{10}$ of a dollar = \$

4. Two dollars plus $\frac{3}{10}$ of a dollar = \$

5. Two dollars plus two tenths of a dollar = \$

6. Two tenths plus seven hundredths of a dollar = \$

7. $\frac{5}{10} + \frac{3}{100}$ of a dollar = \$

8. Ten dollars plus $\frac{5}{100}$ of a dollar = \$

9. Three dollars plus $\frac{3}{100}$ of a dollar = \$

10. $\frac{9}{10} + \frac{9}{100}$ of a dollar = \$

Note for parent: Remind your child that numbers to the left of the decimal point are whole dollars and numbers to the right are cents or fractions of a dollar.

Money: Fractional Values

Write the missing values. The first one has been done for you.

1. 1¢ penny = 1 cent = $\frac{1}{100}$

2. 5¢ nickel = $\square$ cents = $\frac{\square}{100}$ = $\frac{\square}{20}$

3. 10¢ dime = $\square$ cents = $\frac{\square}{100}$ = $\frac{\square}{10}$

4. 25¢ quarter = $\square$ cents = $\frac{\square}{100}$ = $\frac{1}{\square}$

Find the total of the coins and then write the fractional values.

1. 10¢ 10¢ = $\square$ ¢ = $\frac{\square}{100}$ = $\frac{\square}{5}$ of a dollar

2. 25¢ 25¢ = $\square$ ¢ = $\frac{\square}{100}$ = $\frac{1}{\square}$ of a dollar

3. 25¢ 25¢ 10¢ = $\square$ ¢ = $\frac{\square}{100}$ = $\frac{\square}{10}$ = $\frac{\square}{\square}$ of a dollar

4. 25¢ 25¢ 10¢ 10¢ 5¢ = $\square$ ¢ = $\frac{\square}{100}$ = $\frac{\square}{4}$ of a dollar

5. 25¢ 25¢ 10¢ 10¢ 10¢ = $\square$ ¢ = $\frac{\square}{100}$ = $\frac{\square}{5}$ of a dollar

Note for parent: Coins are a practical way of demonstrating fractional values.

Money: Fractions and Decimals

Complete the table. Work across the rows by adding up the money in the left-hand column then filling in the columns to the right.

Remember:

 1 penny = $\frac{1}{100}$ = \$0.01

 1 nickel = $\frac{5}{100}$ = \$0.05

 1 dime = $\frac{10}{100}$ = \$0.10

 1 quarter = $\frac{25}{100}$ = \$0.25

Money Total	As a Fraction	As a Decimal
	$\frac{5}{100}$	
		\$0.75
	$1\frac{25}{100}$	
		\$0.39
		\$2.15

Note for parent: Coins help children visualize fractional values of money.

Change Fractions to Decimals

Remember: $\frac{1}{10} = 0.1$ $\frac{1}{100} = 0.01$ $\frac{1}{1{,}000} = 0.001$

Mixed numbers: $1\frac{1}{10} = 1.1$ $1\frac{1}{100} = 1.01$ $1\frac{1}{1{,}000} = 1.001$

Convert these mixed number fractions to decimal numbers.

$1\frac{1}{10} = 1.1$ We say, **"One and one tenth."**

1. $3\frac{1}{10} =$ ☐
2. $4\frac{5}{10} =$ ☐
3. $9\frac{7}{10} =$ ☐
4. $8\frac{6}{10} =$ ☐

$1\frac{1}{100} = 1.01$ We say, **"One and one hundredth."**

5. $2\frac{5}{100} =$ ☐
6. $3\frac{1}{100} =$ ☐
7. $9\frac{50}{100} =$ ☐
8. $10\frac{20}{100} =$ ☐

$1\frac{1}{1{,}000} = 1.001$ We say, **"One and one thousandth."**

9. $2\frac{1}{1{,}000} =$ ☐
10. $3\frac{2}{1{,}000} =$ ☐
11. $3\frac{15}{1{,}000} =$ ☐
12. $6\frac{25}{1{,}000} =$ ☐

Note for parent: Remembering place value after the decimal point is not easy and will require a lot of practice at this stage.

Use Division to Change Fractions

We can convert fractions to decimals using regular division.
If we want to convert $\frac{3}{5}$ to a decimal number we can do it this way:

$\frac{3}{5} = 3 \div 5$ Remember: $\frac{3}{5}$ ← 3: dividend (or numerator); ← 5: divisor (or denominator)

Short division:

$$5\overline{)3^{3}.0} = 0.6$$

← 3 as a decimal = 3.0

$\frac{3}{5} = 0.6$

Step 1:
We can't divide 3 by 5 so we change 3 to a decimal number. Note the value of the 3 stays the same.

Step 2:
Write the decimal point on the answer line directly above.

Step 3:
Exchange 3 units for 30 tenths. How many 5s in 30 tenths?

Try these yourself. Use **short division**.

1. $\frac{9}{10} = 9 \div$ ☐ $10\overline{)9.0}$ ☐

2. $\frac{3}{4} = 3 \div$ ☐ $4\overline{)3.00}$ ☐

3. $\frac{1}{4} = 1 \div$ ☐ $4\overline{)1.00}$ ☐

4. $\frac{1}{2} = 1 \div$ ☐ $2\overline{)1.0}$ ☐

Note for parent: Children need to understand that 3, 3.0, and 3.000000 are the same value. The number stays the same no matter how many zeros we write after the decimal point.

Try this example using **long division**. Some numbers have been put in already to help you.

1. $\frac{3}{8} = 3 \div \square$

```
       [    ]
    8 | 3.0 0 0
    – 2 4
        6 0
    –
    
    –
```

Step 1: We can't divide 3 by 8 evenly so we change 3 to a decimal number.

Step 2: How many 8s in 30? 3 remainder 6.

Step 3: How many 8s in 60? 7 remainder 4.

Step 4: How many 8s in 40? 5 with no remainder.

$\frac{3}{8} = 0.375$

We say, "Three hundred seventy-five thousandths."

Try these yourself. Some numbers have been put in already to help you.

2. $\frac{5}{8} = 5 \div 8$

```
        0.6
    8 | 5.0 0 0
    – 4 8
        2 0
    –
    
    –
```

$\frac{5}{8} = \square$

3. $\frac{7}{8} = 7 \div 8$

```
       [    ]
    8 | 7.0 0 0
    – 6 4
    
    –
    
    –
```

$\frac{7}{8} = \square$

Length Conversions

Length is a measurement of something from end to end. We can measure length in customary units. Remember these conversions:

12 inches (in.) = 1 foot (ft.)
3 feet = 1 yard (yd.)
36 inches = 1 yard (yd.)
1,760 yards = 1 mile (mi.)

When we convert measurements from one unit of measure to another we have to decide whether we need to multiply or divide.

- When we go from a *larger* unit (e.g., feet) to a smaller unit (e.g., inches) we *multiply*.
- When we go from a *smaller* unit (e.g., inches) to a larger unit (e.g., feet) we *divide*.

1. How do we convert 6 feet to inches?
We know that feet are *larger* than inches so we *multiply*.

6 x 12 = ☐ in.

Multiply by 12 to convert to inches.

2. How do we convert 48 inches to feet?
We know that inches are *smaller* than feet so we *divide*.

48 ÷ 12 = ☐ ft.

Divide by 12 to convert to feet.

Convert these measurements.

3. 60 in. = ☐ ft. → because 60 ÷ 12 = ☐
4. 10 ft. = ☐ in. → because 10 x 12 = ☐
5. 15 yd. = ☐ ft. → because 15 x ☐ = ☐
6. 99 ft. = ☐ yd. → because 99 ÷ ☐ = ☐

Note for parent: We want children to realize that when we multiply in a conversion we get a greater number of units, but when we divide the result is fewer units.

Length Word Problems

Figure out the answers to these two-step problems.

Step 1: Convert different measurements to the same measurements.

Step 2: Add, subtract, multiply, or divide to solve the problem.

Use a separate piece of paper for your work.

1. I have a set of four photos. Each photo is 6 inches wide. I want to put them in a frame side by side. What width in feet does my frame need to be?

   My frame needs to be ____ ft. wide.

2. A roll of tape is 6 yards long. If I use half of the tape, how much is left in inches?

   ____ in. of tape is left.

3. A ladder is 25 feet long and it can be extended by another 36 inches. What is the total length of the ladder in feet?

   The total length of the ladder is ____ ft.

4. The store is a quarter of a mile from my house and José's house is another 500 yards farther. How far in yards is José's house from my house?

   José's house is ____ yd. from my house.

Note for parent: Remind children of the need to convert different measurements to the same measurements.

Metric Length Conversions

We can measure length in metric units. Remember these conversions:

"centi" means $\frac{1}{100}$ and "milli" means $\frac{1}{1{,}000}$

10 millimeters (mm) = 1 centimeter (cm)
100 centimeters = 1 meter (m)
1,000 meters = 1 kilometer (km)

1. How do we convert 1.5 cm to mm? We know that centimeters are *larger* than millimeters so we *multiply*.

1.5 cm = 15 mm

Multiply by 10 to convert to millimeters. The decimal point moves 1 place to the right.

2. How we convert 5 cm to m? We know that centimeters are *smaller* than meters so we *divide*.

5. cm = 0.05 m

Divide by 100 to convert to meters. The decimal point moves 2 places to the left.

Convert these measurements:

3. 6 m = ☐ cm
4. 16.5 cm = ☐ mm
5. 0.6 km = ☐ m
6. 6,000 m = ☐ km

Sometimes we need to add one or more zeros as placeholders when we move a decimal point. If there is no decimal point shown, it is at the end of the number.

Note for parent: You can refer to the previous section for a refresh of decimal multiplication and decimal division.

Metric Length Word Problems

Figure out the answers to these two-step problems. Use a separate piece of paper for your work.

Remember to convert different units of measure to the same units of measure.

1. Rory is building a rabbit hutch for his pet rabbit. He has a piece of wood that measures 1.45 meters long. He needs to cut this to 122 centimeters for the frame. How much wood does he cut off? Write your answer in centimeters.

He cuts off ☐ cm.

2. Amir's desk is 110 centimeters long. It fits against a wall that is 2 meters long. His new bookcase is 0.5 meters long. If he puts his bookcase next to his desk how much space will be left? Write your answer in centimeters.

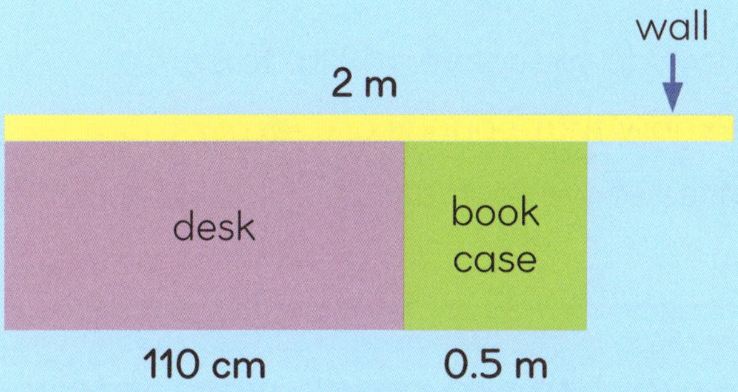

There will be ☐ cm of space left.

3. Tasha runs 5.2 kilometers on Saturday, and 5,600 meters on Sunday. How much farther does she run on Sunday? Write your answer in kilometers.

She runs ☐ km farther.

Note for parent: Drawing a diagram will help children to visualize the steps they need to take in order to solve the problem.

Weight Conversions

Weight (or mass) is a measurement of how heavy something is. We can measure weight in customary units. Remember these conversions:

16 ounces (oz.) = 1 pound (lb.)   2,000 pounds (lb.) = 1 ton (tn.)

1. How do we convert 20 oz. to lb.?
We know that ounces are *smaller* than pounds so we *divide*.

20 ÷ 16 = ☐ lb. ☐ oz.

Divide by 16 to convert to pounds.

---

2. How do we convert 12 lb. to oz.?
We know that pounds are *larger* than ounces so we *multiply*.

12 x 16 = ☐ oz.

Multiply by 16 to convert to ounces.

Convert these measurements.

3. 50 lb. = ☐ oz. → because 50 x 16 = ☐
4. 96 oz. = ☐ lb. → because 96 ÷ 16 = ☐
5. 6 tn. = ☐ lb. → because 6 x ☐ = ☐
6. 8,000 lb. = ☐ tn. → because 8,000 ÷ ☐ = ☐
7. 224 oz. = ☐ lb. → because 224 ÷ ☐ = ☐
8. 25 tn. = ☐ lb. → because 25 x ☐ = ☐

Note for parent: Always encourage your child to check if their answers sound reasonable by using a rough estimate.

Weight Word Problems

Figure out the answers to these multi-step problems.
Use a separate piece of paper for your work.

1. Two adult elephants each weigh 3 tons, and their three young elephants each weigh 2,000 pounds. What is the total weight of the family of elephants in tons?

The family weighs ☐ tn. in total.

2. A newborn baby kitten weighs on average 4 ounces, a newborn human baby weighs on average 8 pounds, and a newborn baby elephant weighs around 216 pounds. How many times heavier is the baby elephant than the human baby? How many times heavier is the human baby than the baby kitten?

The baby elephant is ☐ times heavier than the human baby.

The human baby is ☐ times heavier than the baby kitten.

3. An adult elephant needs to eat up to 300 pounds of grasses, roots, and bark each day to remain healthy.

a) How many tons of food will an adult elephant need to eat in a week? Is your answer nearer to 1 ton or 2 tons? Check ✔ the correct answer.

1 tn. ☐ 2 tn. ☐

b) Which bag of food will feed an adult elephant for one day? Check ✔ the correct answer.

400 oz. ☐ 4,000 oz. ☐ 4,800 oz. ☐

Note for parent: Comparing different weights will help children see that numbers have meaning.

Metric Weight Conversions

We can measure weight in metric units. Remember this conversion:

1,000 grams (g) = 1 kilogram (kg)

1. How do we convert 7.5 kg to g? 7.5 = 7,500 g

We multiply by 1,000 to convert to grams so we move the decimal point 3 places to the right, and add 2 zeros as placeholders. We don't need to put the decimal point at the end of the number.

2. How we convert 7,500 g to kg? 7,500 g = 7.5 kg

We divide by 1,000 to convert to kilograms so the decimal point moves 3 places to the left.

3. How do we convert 5,000 g to kg? We know that grams are *smaller* than kilograms so we *divide*.

5,000 ÷ 1,000 = ☐ kg

Divide by 1,000 to convert to kilograms.

4. How do we convert 7 kg to g? We know that kilograms are *larger* than grams so we *multiply*.

7 x 1,000 = ☐ g

Multiply by 1,000 to convert to grams.

Convert these measurements.

5. 6 kg = ☐ g

6. 4,000 g = ☐ kg

7. 5.5 kg = ☐ g

8. 3,500 g = ☐ kg

Note for parent: Always encourage your child to check if the answers sound reasonable, using a rough estimate.

Metric Weight Word Problems

Figure out the answers to these multi-step problems. Use a separate piece of paper for your work.

1. If a pineapple weighs 1 kilogram, a watermelon weighs 1.2 kilograms, and a bunch of bananas weighs 500 grams, what is the total weight of the fruit all together?

All together the fruit weighs ☐ kg.

2. Convert the weights to grams and find the total.

3 pineapples at 1 kg each = ☐ g

4 watermelons at 1.2 kg each = ☐ g

2 bunches of bananas at 500 g each = ☐ g

Total weight = ☐ g

3. If one apple weighs 150 grams, how much do 8 apples weigh? Circle the correct answer.

1.2 kg

1.3 kg

1.1 kg

4. If one orange weighs 250 grams and I buy a bag of oranges weighing 2.5 kilograms in total, how many oranges do I have? Circle the correct answer.

10 15 20

Capacity Conversions

Capacity is a measurement of how much something holds. We can measure capacity in customary units. Remember these conversions:

8 fluid ounces (fl. oz.) = 1 cup (c.)
2 cups = 1 pint (pt.)
2 pints = 4 cups, or 1 quart (qt.)
4 quarts = 1 gallon (gal.)

Try to visualize how many of these customary units are equal to 1 gallon.

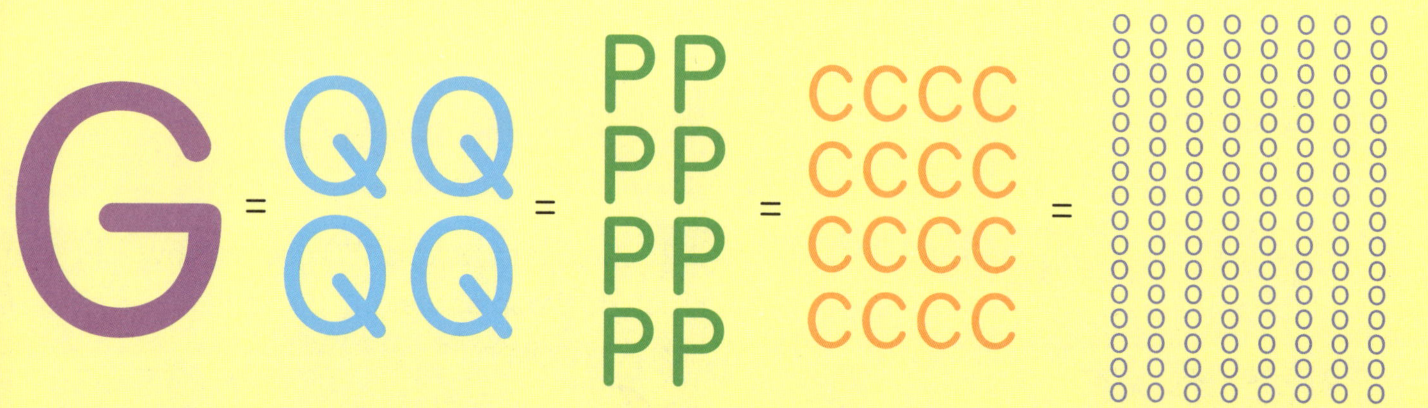

1 gallon = 4 quarts = 8 pints = 16 cups = 128 fluid ounces

Use the model above to convert these measurements.

1. 3 gal. = ☐ pt.

8 pt. = 1 gal. so we multiply 3 x 8

2. 3 qt. = ☐ c.

3. 10 gal. = ☐ qt.

4. $\frac{1}{2}$ gal. = ☐ pt.

5. 32 c. = ☐ gal.

6. 32 pt. = ☐ gal.

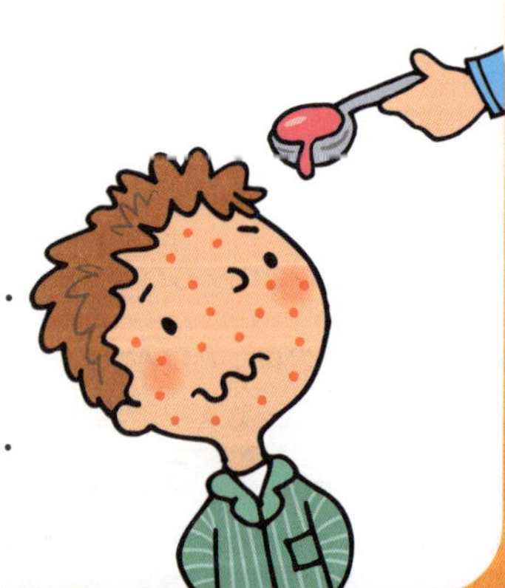

Note for parent: Some children will find pictures, such as the capacity model above, easier to remember than facts.

Capacity Word Problems

Figure out the answers to these multi-step problems. You may need to add, subtract, multiply and/or divide to find the answers. Use a separate piece of paper for your work.

1. The school hockey teams has 12 pints of juice for refreshment after the game.

How many players can have 1 cup of juice? ☐ players can have 1 cup each.

How many players can have 2 cups of juice? ☐ players can have 2 cups each.

2. The 20 guests at Jack's party each drink 3 cups of soda. How many quarts of soda is this in total?

Total = ☐ qt.

3. A camel can drink 53 gallons of water in one sitting! How much is this in cups?

Total = ☐ c.

4. Mrs. Ramirez waters her potted plants once a day in the hot summer months. She gives each of her 6 plants $1\frac{1}{2}$ pints at each watering. How much water is this in gallons per week? Is it nearer 8 gallons, or nearer 9 gallons? Circle your answer.

8 gallons   9 gallons

Note for parent: You could think up more math problems such as these to give your child further practice.

Metric Capacity Conversions

We can measure capacity in metric units. Remember these conversions:

500 milliliters (mL) = 0.5 liter (L)
1,000 milliliters (mL) = 1 liter (L)

Study this conversion table:

Quantity in mL	Quantity in L	As a Fraction
250 mL	0.25 L	$\frac{1}{4}$ L
500 mL	0.50 L	$\frac{1}{2}$ L
750 mL	0.75 L	$\frac{3}{4}$ L
1,000 mL	1 L	$\frac{1}{1}$ L

Remember 0.50 and 0.5 have the same value. Sometimes we write 0.50 with 0 as a placeholder after the 5 for column calculations and tables.

Try to work out these conversions for yourself:

Quantity in mL	Quantity in L	As a Fraction
100 mL	0.10 L	
200 mL		$\frac{2}{10}$ L or $\frac{1}{5}$ L
300 mL		$\frac{3}{10}$ L
400 mL	0.40 L	
800 mL		$\frac{8}{10}$ L or $\frac{4}{5}$ L
1,100 mL		$1\frac{1}{10}$ L

Note for parent: It is useful to think about real-world comparisons. For example, a drip from a tap is about a milliliter, and two small bottles of water are approximately a liter.

Metric Capacity Word Problems

Figure out the answers to these multi-step problems. You may need to add, subtract, multiply, and/or divide to find the answers. Use a separate piece of paper for your work.

1. A full bucket holds 3 liters of water. A full pitcher holds 750 milliliters. How many pitchers full of water are needed to fill the bucket?

☐ pitchers full are needed.

2. How many milliliters of milk must be added to 2.2 liters to make 5 liters all together?

☐ mL must be added.

3. A small can of paint contains 200 milliliters. There is four and a half times as much paint in a larger can. How much paint is in the larger can? Is this amount greater than (**>**) or less than (**<**) a liter?

In a larger can there is ☐ mL of paint. This is ☐ than a liter.

4. A vet wants to share 2.4 liters of water equally among 12 puppies. How many milliliters of water will each puppy receive?

Each puppy will receive ☐ mL of water.

Note for parent: This activity brings together what children have learned about fractions, decimals, and measurement from this book so far.

Time Conversions

Remember these units of time:

60 seconds = 1 minute (min.)
24 hours = 1 day
60 minutes = 1 hour (hr.)
7 days = 1 week

365 days = 1 year
100 years = 1 century
10 years = 1 decade

Answer these problems by multiplying to convert time.

1. How many seconds in an hour?

What is 60 seconds multiplied by 60?

	T	U
	6	0
x	6	0

2. How many minutes are there in a day?

What is 60 minutes multiplied by 24?

	T	U
	6	0
x	2	4

3. How many hours in a year? 24 x 365 days = ☐

What is 24 hours multiplied by 365 days?

	300	60	5
20	6,000		
4			

6,000 + ☐ + ☐ + ☐ + ☐ + ☐ = ☐

Note for parent: Time conversions can be tricky because the numbers involved are not so easy to handle.

Elapsed Time—Using an Analog Clock

Elapsed time is time that passes between the start of an activity and the end of an activity.

Remember: **a.m.** in Latin "ante meridiem" means *before* midday
p.m. in Latin "post meridiem" means *after* midday

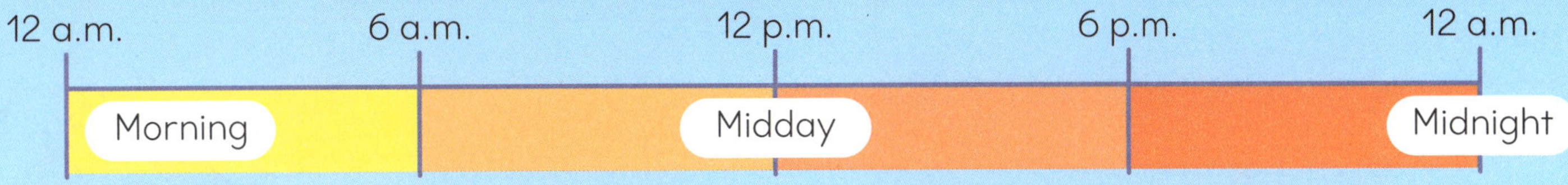

For smaller calculations of time, you can figure out time problems mentally by counting forward and backward on an analog clock.

1. Al went to his swimming lesson. He left at 9:40 a.m. and arrived home 1 hour and 50 minutes later. What time did he arrive home?

Count forward 1 hour and 50 minutes in steps:

Step 1: Count forward 1 hour from 9:40 = ___ : ___ a.m.

Step 2: Count forward 20 minutes up to the next hour = ___ : ___ a.m.

Step 3: Count forward the remaining 30 minutes = ___ : ___ a.m.

Answer: ___ : ___ a.m.

2. Gemma spends 1 hour and 40 minutes at a friend's party. If the party ends at 4:30 p.m. what time did the party start?

Count back 1 hour and 40 minutes in steps:

Step 1: Count back 1 hour from 4:30 = ___ : ___ p.m.

Step 2: Count back 30 minutes to the previous hour = ___ : ___ p.m.

Step 3: Count back the remaining 10 minutes = ___ : ___ p.m.

Answer: ___ : ___ p.m.

Note for parent: This method of counting around the clockface works well with shorter amounts of time where children are able to add and subtract time mentally.

Graphing Data on Line Plots

Mia collected data to find out how much rain fell over a period of 14 days. Graph Mia's data in a line plot. Write an X on the line plot to represent the amount of rain on the inches scale.

Day 1	Day 2	Day 3	Day 4	Day 5	Day 6	Day 7
1	1	$1\frac{1}{2}$	$\frac{1}{2}$	$1\frac{3}{4}$	$1\frac{1}{4}$	0
Day 8	**Day 9**	**Day 10**	**Day 11**	**Day 12**	**Day 13**	**Day 14**
0	$1\frac{3}{4}$	$\frac{1}{2}$	$2\frac{1}{4}$	$1\frac{1}{2}$	4	4

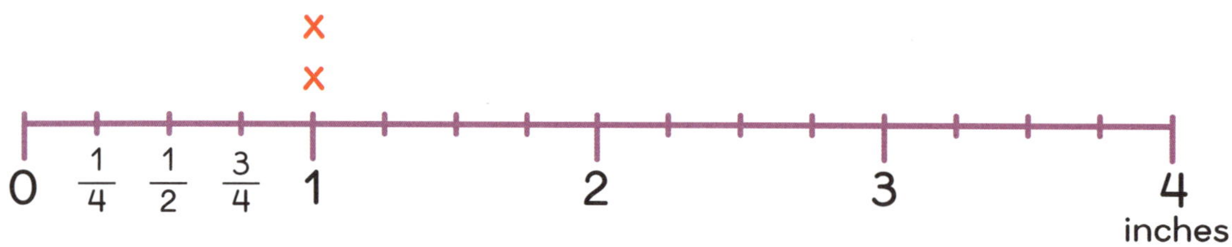

Answer these questions by studying the data in the your completed line plot.

1. What was the most rain to fall in one day? .... in.
2. How many days had no rainfall? .... days
3. How many days had 2 or more inches of rain? .... days
4. How much rain fell in total over the 14 days? .... in.

Add together all the amounts. Group the numbers to make addition easier:

Super-challenging question!

$$\underbrace{1 + 1 + 1\frac{1}{2} + \frac{1}{2}}_{4} + \underbrace{1\frac{3}{4} + 1\frac{1}{4}}_{3} + \underbrace{1\frac{3}{4} + \frac{1}{2}}_{2\frac{1}{4}} + \underbrace{2\frac{1}{4} + 1\frac{1}{2}}_{3\frac{3}{4}} + \underbrace{4 + 4}_{8} =$$

$$4 + 3 + 2\frac{1}{4} + 3\frac{3}{4} + 8 =$$

Now regroup again:

$$\underbrace{4 + 3}_{7} + \underbrace{2\frac{1}{4} + 3\frac{3}{4}}_{6} + 8 =$$

$$7 + 6 + 8 = \square$$

Note for parent: A line plot is a useful visual means of displaying scientific and mathematical data.

This table lists the lengths of 11 tadpoles in a garden pond. Graph the data in a line plot. Write an X on the line plot to represent the length of each tadpole on the inches scale.

$\frac{1}{4}$	$\frac{1}{2}$	1	$1\frac{1}{2}$	$1\frac{1}{2}$	$\frac{3}{4}$	1	1	$\frac{3}{4}$	1	$\frac{3}{4}$

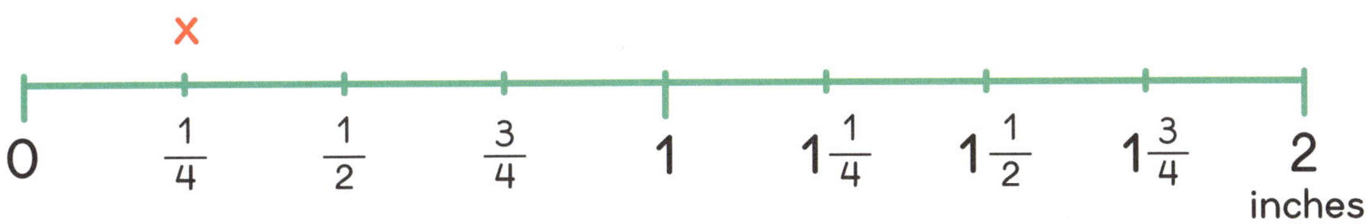

Answer these questions by studying the data in the your completed line plot.

1. What length is the longest tadpole? .... in.

2. What is the length of the shortest tadpole? .... in.

3. What is the difference in length between the longest tadpole and the shortest tadpole? .... in.

4. If all the tadpoles swam in a long line, head to tail, how long would the line of tadpoles be? .... in.

Super-challenging calculation!

Add together all the amounts. Group the numbers to make addition easier:

$$\left(\frac{1}{4} + \frac{1}{2}\right) + \left(\frac{3}{4} \times 3\right) + (1 \times 4) + \left(1\frac{1}{2} \times 2\right) =$$

$$\frac{3}{4} + 2\frac{1}{4} + 4 + 3 = \square$$

5. If a fish ate half of this line of tadpoles, what length would be left? .... in.

Calculate and Classify Angles

Angles are formed when something rotates around a point. When you open this book an angle is formed at the spine.

Angles are measured in units called degrees. Remember these facts:

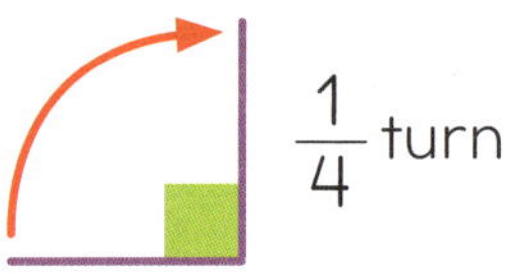

Right angle = 90°

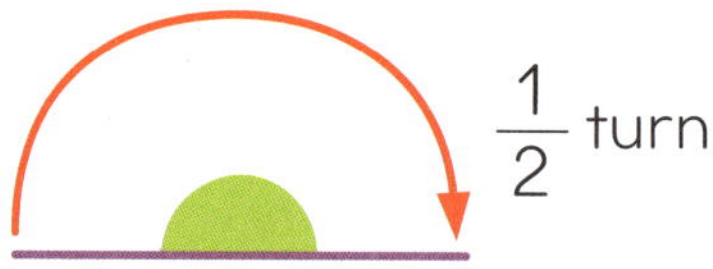

Straight line = 180°

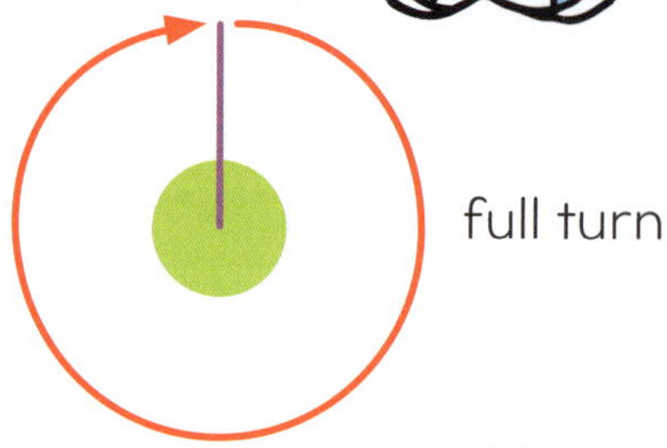

complete rotation = 360°

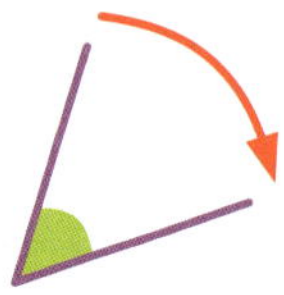

Acute angle = less than 90°

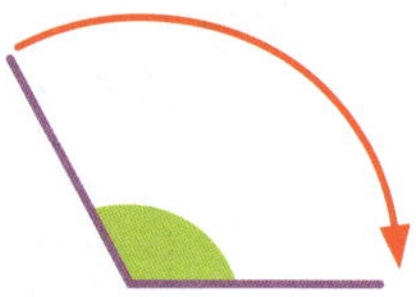

Obtuse angle = between 90° and 180°

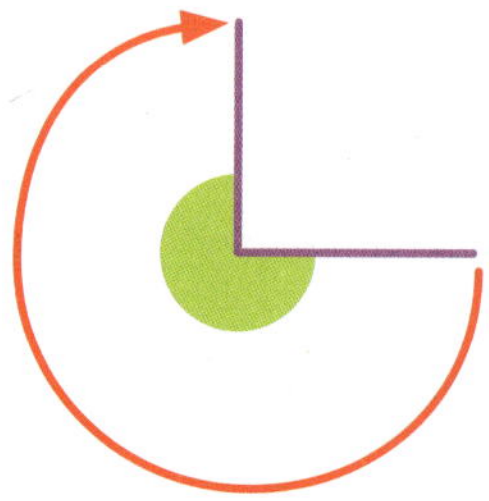

Reflex angle = between 180° and 360°

Calculate the unknown angles (called **n** and **m**), and classify them as either right, acute, or obtuse.

1.

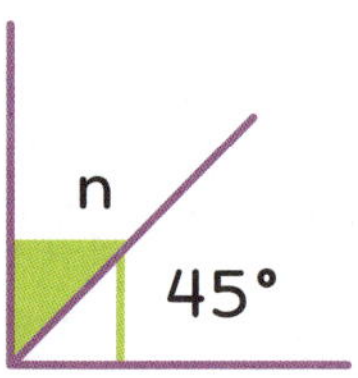

n = ☐ °

n = acute

2.

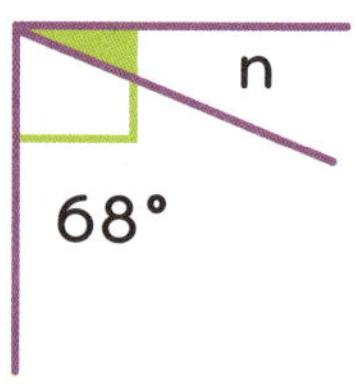

n = ☐ °

n = ...

3.

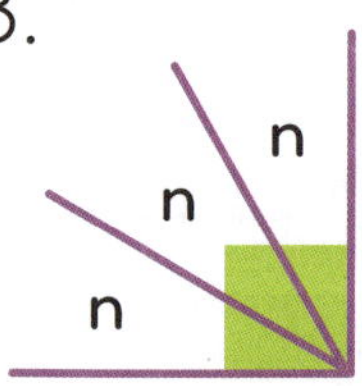

n = ☐ ° n = ...

A square ☐ indicates a right angle.

Note for parent: This activity provides practice in identifying angles and finding the unknown angle.

4.

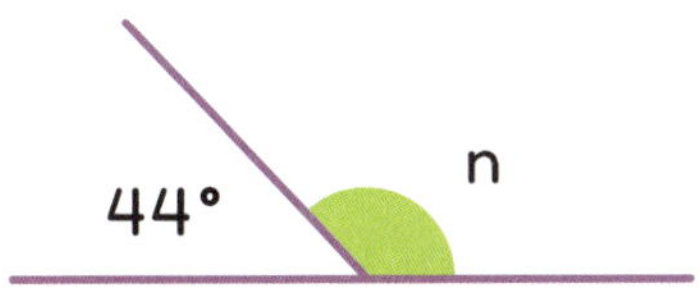

n = ☐ °

n = ...

5.

n = ☐ °

n = ...

6.

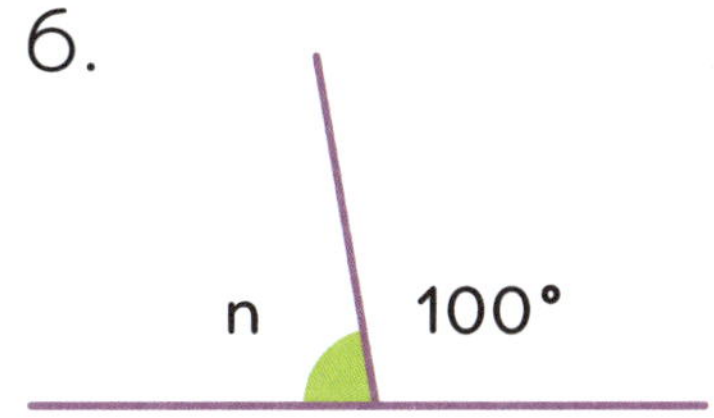

n = ☐ °

n = ...

7.

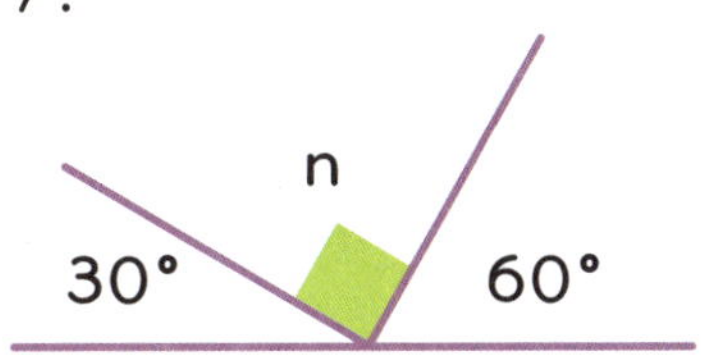

n = ☐ °

n = ...

8.

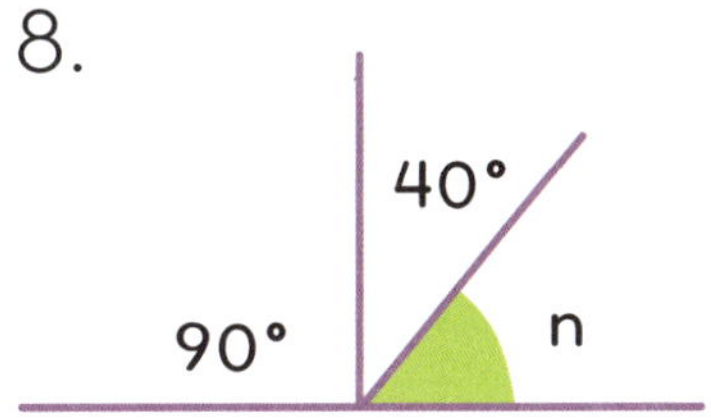

n = ☐ °

n = ...

9.

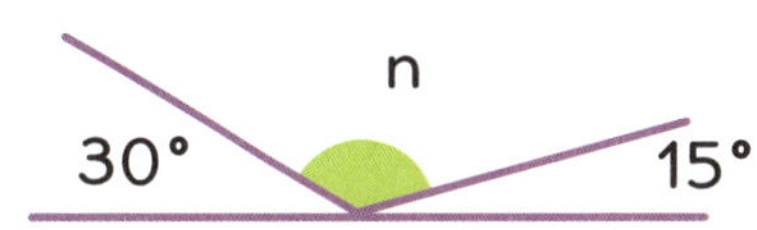

n = ☐ °

n = ...

10.

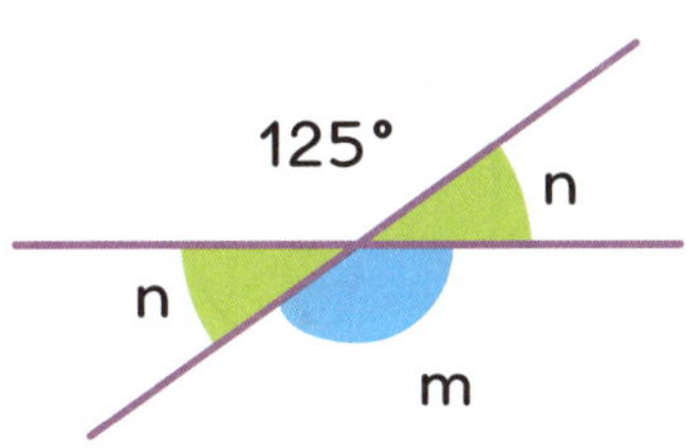

n = ☐ °　　n = ...

m = ☐ °　　m = ...

Parallel and Perpendicular Lines

Parallel lines are the same distance apart all along their length. They never meet or cross each other.

They are marked with arrows on this rhombus below.

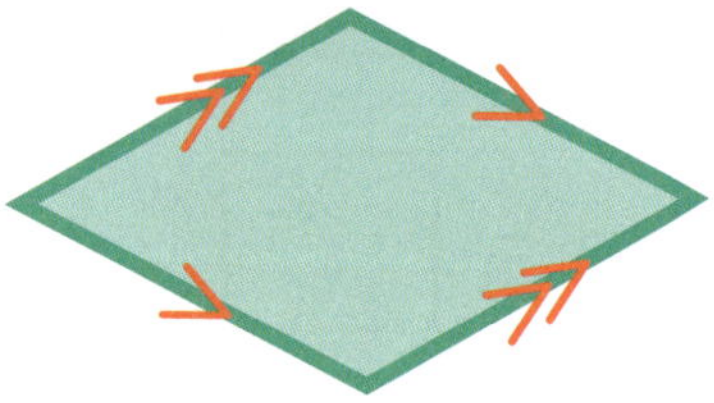

The sides that are parallel are marked with the same number of arrows.

Identify the parallel lines on these shapes and mark with arrows.

trapezoid | trapezoid | square | parallelogram

Perpendicular lines meet or cross at a 90° angle.

You could use the corner of a piece of paper to find right angles in these shapes.

Identify the right angles in these shapes and mark each with a little square.

square | rectangle | right triangle | trapezoid

Note for parent: Look for parallel and perpendicular lines in familiar objects around the home. For example, look at the lines in wall and floor tiling.

Quadrilaterals Family Tree

Study the quadrilaterals family tree then answer the questions below.

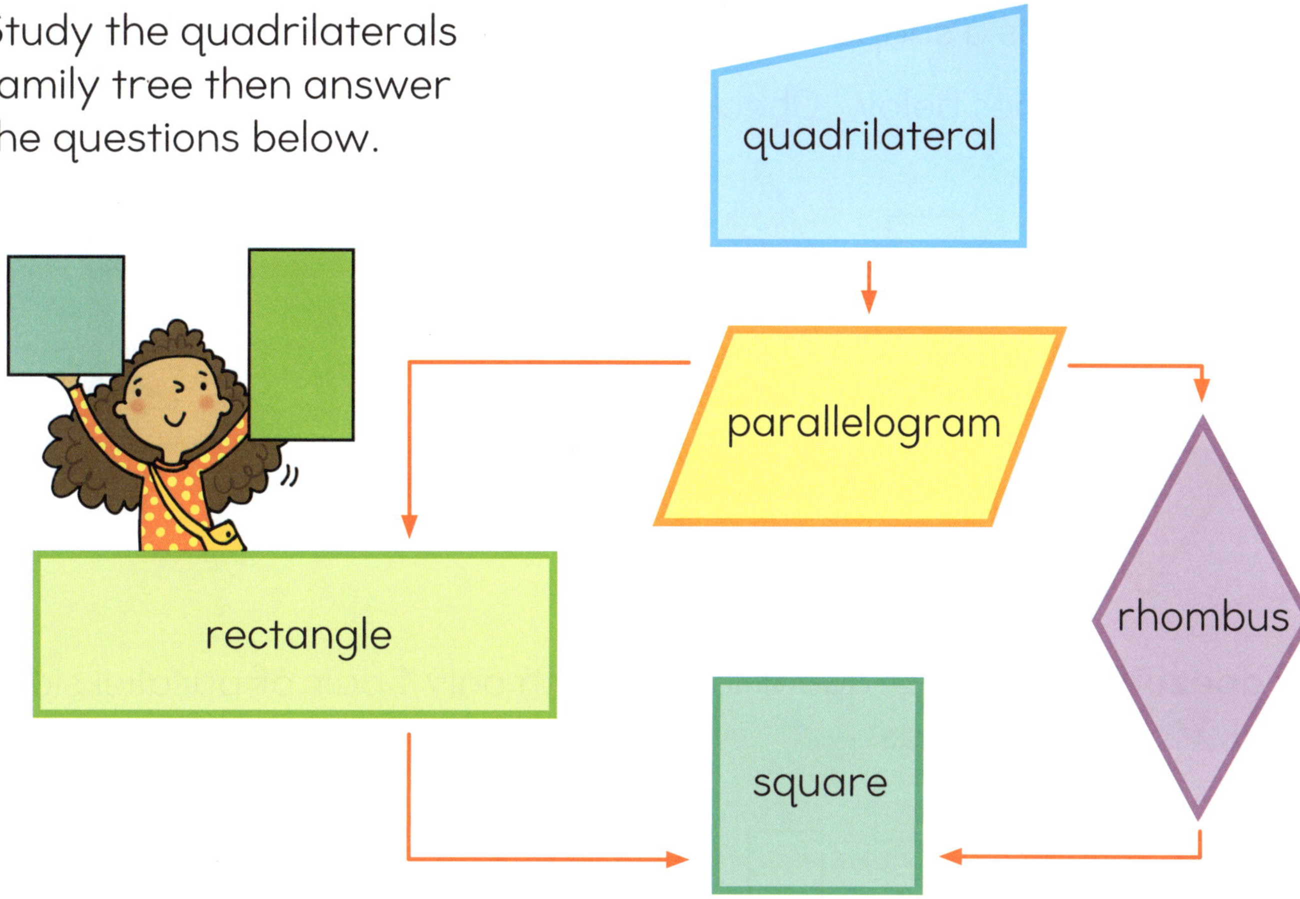

Two of these statements are true and two are false. Write "true" or "false" next to each statement.

1. A quadrilateral has 4 straight sides. ....
2. A parallelogram has only 1 pair of parallel sides. ....
3. A square has 4 sides the same length and only 2 right angles. ....
4. A rectangle has 4 right angles and opposite sides are equal lengths. ....

Now write a true statement for each false statement.

1. ....

2. ....

Note for parent: This activity is a refresh of what children have learned about quadrilaterals so far.

Classifying Quadrilaterals

A **quadrilateral** is a shape with 4 straight sides.

Look at the shapes below. Check ✔ the quadrilaterals.

A **trapezoid** is a type of quadrilateral with only 1 pair of parallel sides. Check ✔ the trapezoids.

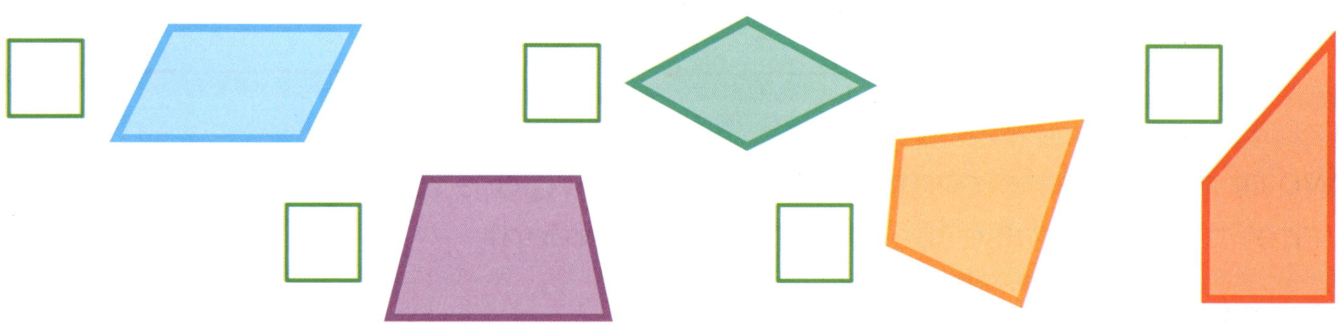

A **parallelogram** is a quadrilateral with 2 pairs of parallel sides. Check ✔ the parallelograms.

Note for parent: Through this activity, children will begin to realize that a shape can belong to more than one group.

A **rhombus** is a type of parallelogram with 4 sides of the same length and equal opposite angles. Check ✔ the rhombuses.

A **rectangle** is a type of parallelogram with 4 right angles. Check ✔ the rectangles.

A **square** is a type of rectangle with 4 sides the same length and 4 right angles. Check ✔ the square.

Perimeter–Including the Unknown Side

The distance all the way around a flat shape is called the **perimeter**.

Calculate the perimeter of these shapes by adding the lengths of all the sides. Start at one corner and go all around the shape.

This is a good place to start.

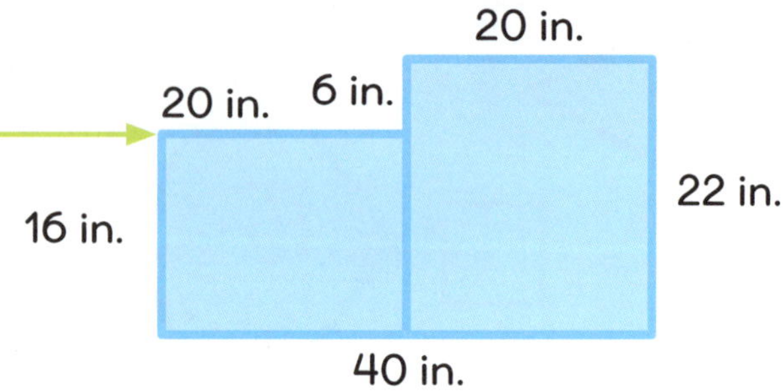

20 + □ + □ + □ + □ + □ = □ in.

These shapes have unknown sides, called **a** and **b**, that you have to figure out before you can find the perimeter.

1. a = 18 − □ a = □

   b = 40 + □ b = □

   40 + 8 + 22 + □ + □ + 18 = □ yd.

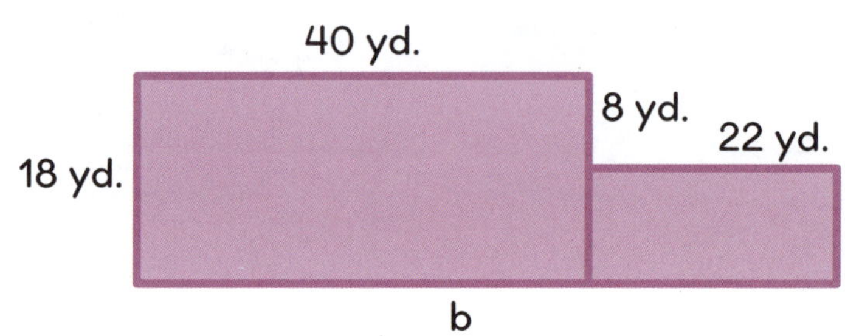

2. a = 66 − □ a = □

   b = 55 − □ b = □

   66 + 55 + 22 + □ + □ + 30 = □ ft.

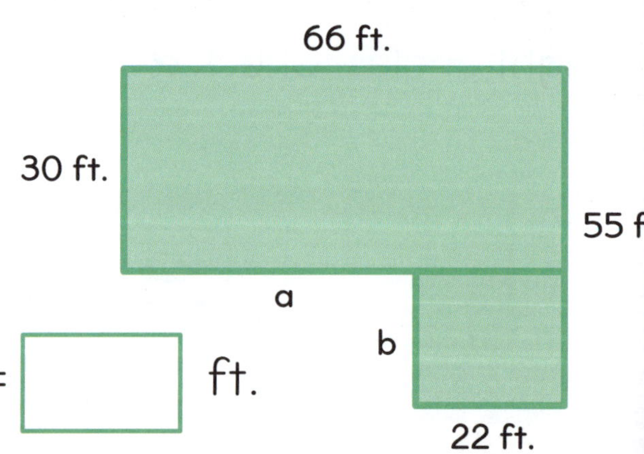

Note for parent: Children can use a calculator to find the perimeter totals if they wish.

The perimeter of a regular polygon (a shape with sides of the same length) is the length of one side multiplied by the total number of sides.

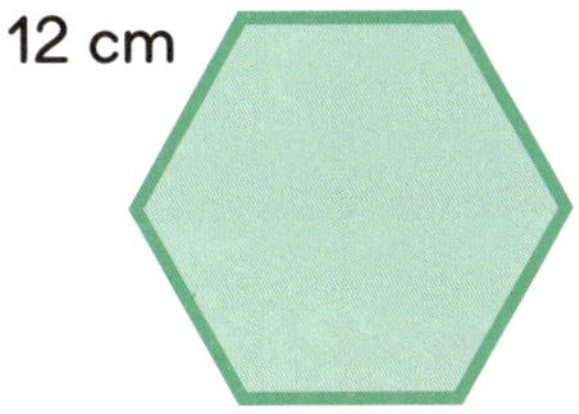

The perimeter of this hexagon is

12 x ☐ = ☐ cm

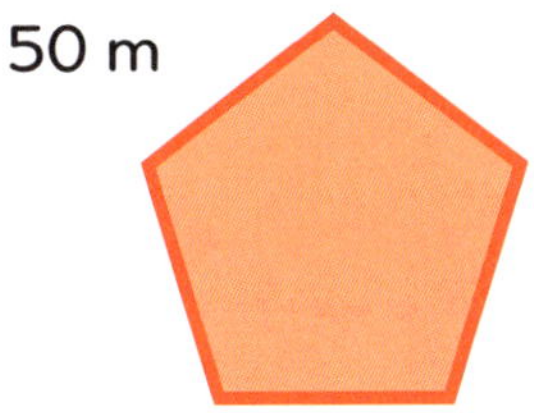

The perimeter of this pentagon is

☐ x ☐ = ☐ m

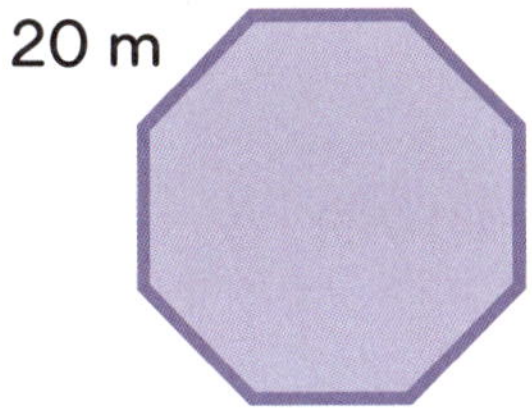

The perimeter of this octagon is

☐ x ☐ = ☐ m

This rectangle has a perimeter of 42 in. It has 3 unknown sides, called **a** and **b**. Figure out the length of **a** and **b**.

Think about what you know about the properties of rectangles. Opposite sides are equal, so we can figure out the value of a.

a = ☐

7 + b + a + b = 42 in.

14 + b + b = 42 in.

42 – ☐ = ☐ in.

b + b = ☐ in.

b = ☐ in.

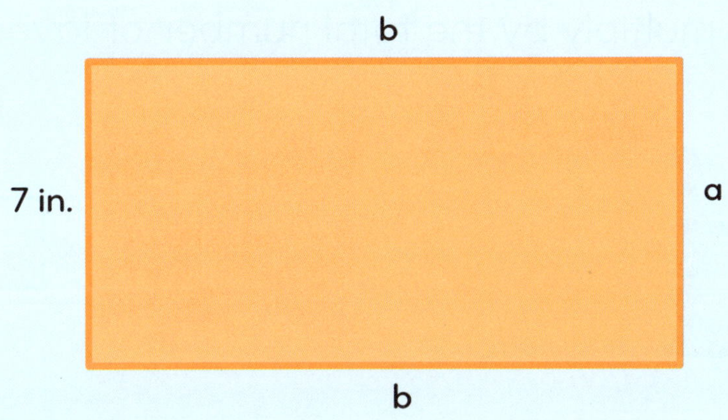

Volume—Cubic Units

Volume is how much space a three-dimensional (3D) object takes up.

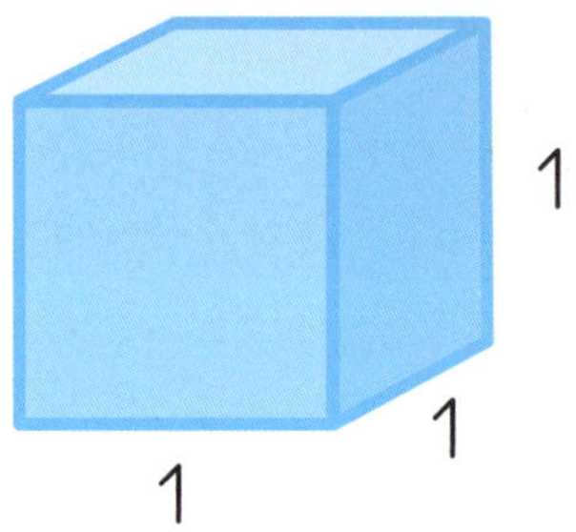

This cube is a 3D object. Each of its sides measures 1 unit so we call it a "unit cube." It has a volume of one cubic unit. We can use it to measure volume.

Look at the 3D shape, A, below. It is made up of layers of cubes, and there are no gaps or overlaps. Count the cubes in the layers to find the volume of the shape.

A

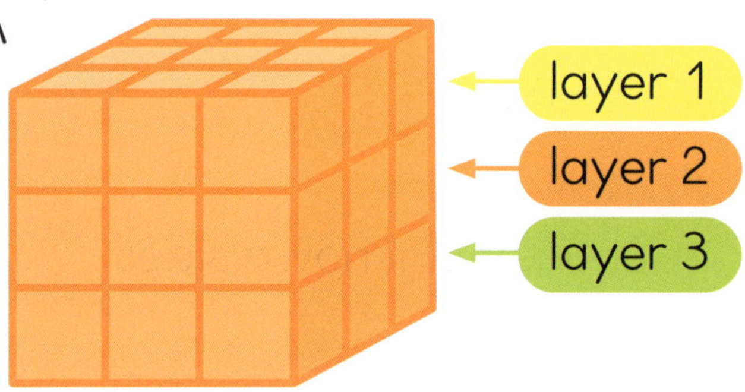

Volume =
layer 1 + layer 2 + layer 3

Volume =

☐ + ☐ + ☐

= ☐ cubic units

Try this prism shape, B. Count how many cubes in the top layer then multiply by the total number of layers.

B

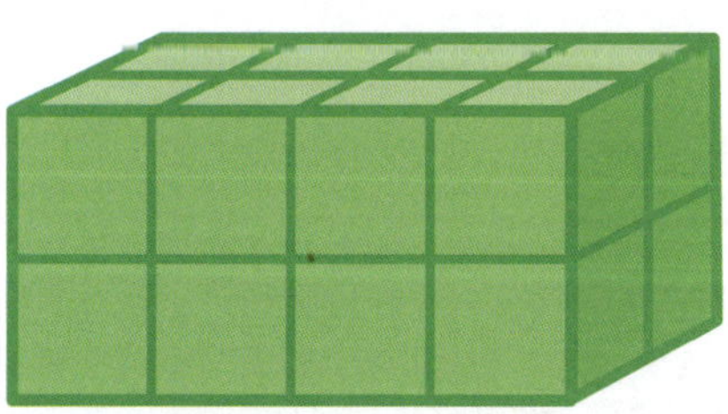

Volume =

☐ x ☐ = ☐ cubic units

Note for parent: Sometimes you will see cubic units (or cu) written as 3 in superscript. For instance, $ft.^3$, m^3, etc.

Sometimes it's not easy to count layers in a 3D shape so we use a formula instead. To find the volume of the containers pictured below we can use this formula:

Volume (V): Multiply the length (l) by the width (w) by the height (h).
We write this as **V = l x w x h**

Try this formula to figure out the volumes of these containers.

1. A cereal box is 20 inches long, by 10 inches wide, by 20 inches high. What is its volume?

Volume =

☐ x ☐ x ☐ = ☐ cubic inches

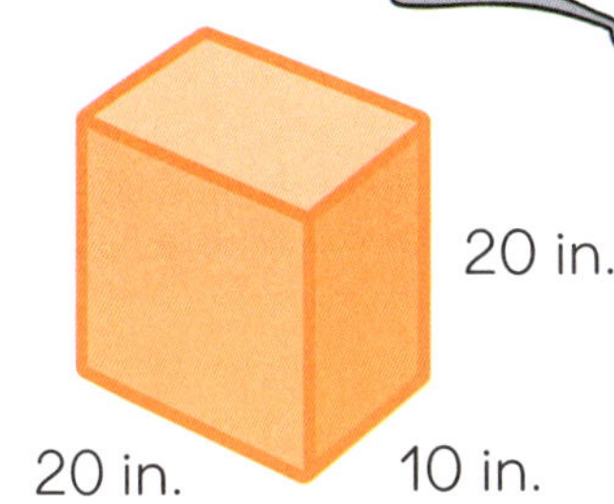

2. A candy box is 5 centimeters long, by 5 centimeters wide, by 15 centimeters high. What is its volume?

Volume =

☐ x ☐ x ☐ = ☐ cubic centimeters

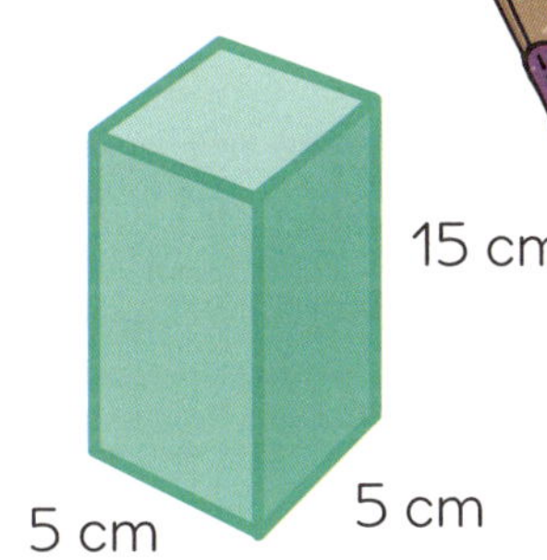

3. A shipping container is 20 feet long, by 8 feet wide, by 8 feet high. What is the volume of the container?

Volume =

☐ x ☐ x ☐ = ☐ cubic feet

Coordinate Problems

Use the coordinates to plot each of these points on the map of the park. Label each one with the letters as shown in the table. The first one has been done for you.

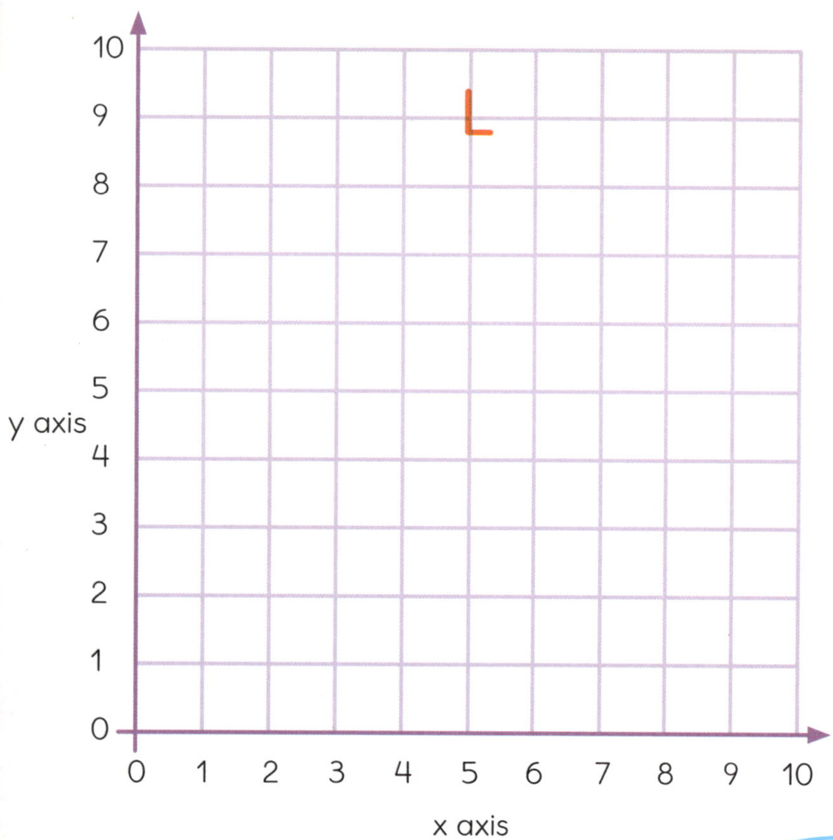

Place (Point)	Coordinates
Lake (**L**)	(5,9)
Sculpture (**S**)	(8,9)
Waterfall (**W**)	(2,8)
Café (**C**)	(6,5)
Flower Garden (**FG**)	(2,3)
Playground (**P**)	(8,3)
Gift Shop (**GS**)	(8,5)
Bridge (**B**)	(5,8)
Picnic Tables (**PT**)	(5,3)

Scale: ☐ = 100 yards

This means the distance between each line on the grid is 100 yards in the real world.

This method of coordinates is also called Cartesian coordinates, invented by René Descartes.

Note for parent: Maps are a real-world example of how we can use coordinates to locate an exact point in a geographical area.

Use the table and the map opposite to answer these questions.

1. How far is it from:

a) The lake to the bridge? .... yards

b) The waterfall to the flower garden? .... yards

c) The flower garden to the playground? .... yards

d) The gift shop to the sculpture? .... yards

2. What will you find halfway between the flower garden and the playground?

....

3. If you are at the sculpture which is nearer: the playground or the lake?

....

4. If you are at the gift shop which is farther away: the sculpture or the playground?

....

5. If you are at the waterfall how much farther away is the flower garden than the bridge?

.... yards

Perimeter and Area Word Problems

Poppy is giving her backyard a makeover and has drawn up a plan. She wants to have a rectangular area of lawn, and around the perimeter of the lawn she wants to plant flowers.

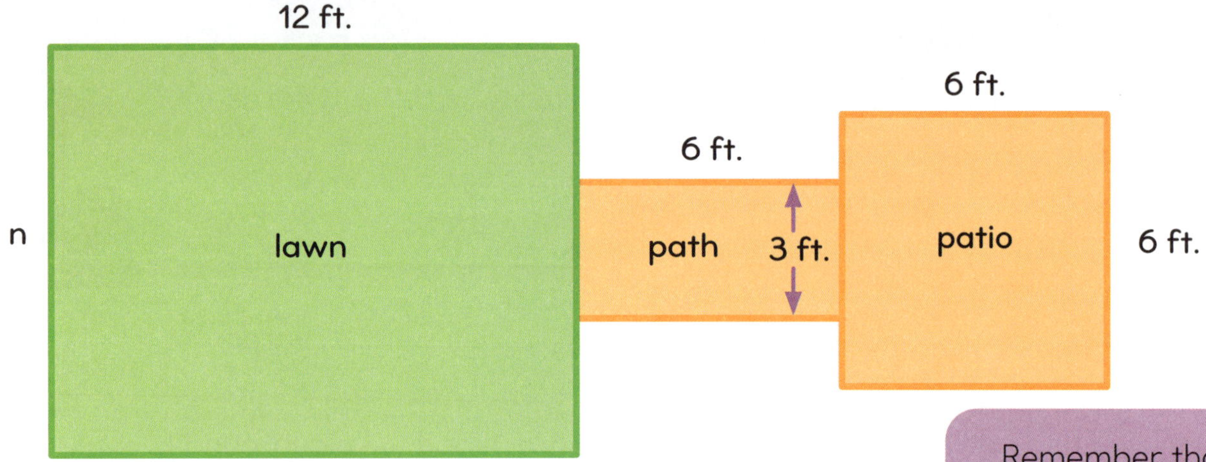

Remember that area = length x width

1. If the area of the lawn is 108 square feet, what is the perimeter?

$12 \times n = 108$ $\quad 108 \div 12 = \square$ $\quad n = \square$ ft.

The perimeter = $\square + \square + \square + \square$ ft. = $\square$ ft.

2. Poppy wants a path from the lawn leading to a square patio. Calculate the total area of the path and the patio.

Area of the path = $\square \times \square = \square$ $ft.^2$

Area of the patio = $\square \times \square = \square$ $ft.^2$

Total area of the path and the patio = $\square + \square = \square$ $ft.^2$

3. Patio tiles are 2 feet by 2 feet, so if Poppy tiled the patio, how many tiles would she need? Use the model to help you.

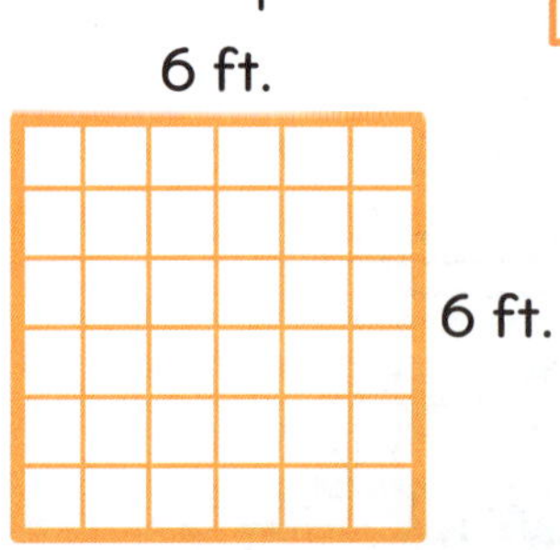

$\square$ tiles

Note for parent: Real-world examples make math concepts more easily understood and relevant to children's lives.

Answers

Page 4

Hundreds	Tens	Units		Tenths	Hundredths	Thousandths
		0	.	0	1	5
		0	.	7		
		7	.	1		
	1	0	.	0	5	
1	1	0	.	0	0	5

Page 5

0.7 > 0.07 0.15 > 0.015
0.8 = 0.80 0.25 < 0.255
0.99 < 1.9 0.091 < 1.901

Pages 6-7

1. $\frac{1}{10}$ 2. $\frac{1}{10}$ 3. $\frac{1}{10}$, $\frac{1}{100}$

4. 10, 1, $\frac{1}{10}$ 5. 10, 1, $\frac{1}{100}$

---

1. 10, $\frac{1}{10}$, $\frac{1}{1000}$ 2. 10, $\frac{1}{10}$, $\frac{1}{1000}$

3. 100, $\frac{1}{10}$, $\frac{1}{100}$

4. 70.75 5. 53.40 6. 680.302

Page 8

3 x 10 = 30 7 x 10 = 70
30 x 10 = 300 70 x 10 = 700
300 x 10 = 3,000 700 x 10 = 7,000

42 x 10 = 420
42 x 100 = 4,200
42 x 1,000 = 42,000

136 x 10 = 1,360
136 x 100 = 13,600
136 x 1,000 = 136,000

Page 9

30 ÷ 10 = 3
300 ÷ 10 = 30
3,000 ÷ 10 = 300

70 ÷ 10 = 7
700 ÷ 10 = 70
7,000 ÷ 10 = 700

650 ÷ 10 = 65
6,500 ÷ 100 = 65
65,000 ÷ 1,000 = 65

1,460 ÷ 10 = 146
14,600 ÷ 100 = 146
146,000 ÷ 1,000 = 146

Pages 10-11

10^2 = 100
10^3 = 1,000
10^4 = 1,000 x 10 = 10,000
10^5 = 10,000 x 10 = 100,000
10^6 = 100,000 x 10 = 1,000,000
3 zeros, 4 zeros, 5 zeros, 6 zeros
10^7 = 10 x 10 x 10 x 10 x 10 x 10 x 10 = 10,000,000
10^8 = 10 x 10 x 10 x 10 x 10 x 10 x 10 x 10 = 100,000,000
10^9 = 10 x 10 x 10 x 10 x 10 x 10 x 10 x 10 x 10 = 1,000,000,000
10^{10} = 10 x 10 x 10 x 10 x 10 x 10 x 10 x 10 x 10 x 10 = 10,000,000,000

Pages 12-13

546 x 26 =

x	500	40	6		
20	10,000	800	120	=	10,920
6	3,000	240	36	=	3,276
				=	14,196

	Th	H	T	U
		2	1 3̸	
		5	4	6
x			2	6
	3,	2	7	6
1	0,	9	2	0
1	4,	1	9	6

427 x 35 =

x	400	20	7		
30	12,000	600	210	=	12,810
5	2,000	100	35	=	2,135
				=	14,945

	Th	H	T	U
		1	2 3̸	
		4	2	7
x			3	5
	2,	1	3	5
1	2,	8	1	0
1	4,	9	4	5

625 x 43 =

x	600	20	5		
40	24,000	800	200	=	25,000
3	1,800	60	15	=	1,875
				=	26,875

	Th	H	T	U
		1	2 1̸	
		6	2	5
x			4	3
	1,	8	7	5
2	5,	0	0	0
2	6,	8	7	5

505 x 26 =

x	500	0	5		
20	10,000	00	100	=	10,100
6	3,000	00	30	=	3,030
				=	13,130

	Th	H	T	U
			1 3̸	
		5	0	5
x			2	6
	3,	0	3	0
1	0,	1	0	0
1	3,	1	3	0

Page 14

22 x 2 = 44
22 x 10 = 220
22 x 20 = 440

Each child gets 22 stickers.

x	20	2
22	440	44

484 − 440 = 44

44 − 44 = 0

Answers

Page 15

The problem could be written as 630 ÷ 15.

15 x 2 = 30
15 x 10 = 150
15 x 20 = 300
15 x 40 = 600

x	40	2
15	600	30

630 − 600 = 30; 30 − 30 = 0

42 minibuses will be needed.

The problem could be writen as 552 ÷ 24.

24 x 2 = 48
24 x 10 = 240
24 x 20 = 480

x	20	2	1
24	480	48	24

552 − 480 = 72; 72 − 48 = 24; 24 − 24 = 0

There are 23 rows of people.

Pages 16-17

1. 25 2. 5
3. 175 4. 560
5. 180 6. 4,215

1. 2,500 2. 52,000
3. 56,700 4. 99,300

1. 100,400 2. 125,900
3. 340,750 4. 503,680
5. 1,709,020

Pages 18-19

1. 0.25 2. 1.73 3. 4.86
4. 3.84 5. 0.52 6. 4.99

1. 0.07 2. 0.15 3. 0.54 4. 5.55

1. 5 3. 0.05
2. 0.5 4. 0.005

Page 20

12.50 + 12.05 = 24.55

H	T	U	.	Ths	Hths
	1	2	.	5	0
	1	2	.	0	5
	2	4	.	5	5

487.19 + 27.82 =

H	T	U	.	Ths	Hths
1	1	1		1	
4	8	7	.	1	9
+	2	7	.	8	2
5	1	5	.	0	1

362.37 + 56.90 =

H	T	U	.	Ths	Hths
1	1				
3	6	2	.	3	7
+	5	6	.	9	0
4	1	9	.	2	7

518.38 + 291.29 =

H	T	U	.	Ths	Hths
1				1	
5	1	8	.	3	8
+2	9	1	.	2	9
8	0	9	.	6	7

Page 21

33.09 + 42.17 = 75.26
93.58 − 21.68 = 71.90

H	T	U	.	Ths	Hths
	1				
	7	1	.	9	0
+	2	1	.	6	8
	9	3	.	5	8

Page 23

8.96 x 4 =

carries: 3 2
8.96
x 4
35.84

Product = 35.84

1.01 x 0.5 =

1.01
x 0.5
505
0000
0.505

Product = 0.505

6.95 x 5.1 =

carries: 4 2
6.95
x 5.1
695
34750
35.445

Product = 35.445

17.45 x 3.2 =

carries: 2 ~~1~~ 1 1 ~~1~~
17.45
x 3.2
3490
52350
55.840

Product = 55.840

Pages 24-25

36.6 ÷ 6 = 6.1 (6)36.6

28.44 ÷ 4 = 7.11 (4)28.44

837.6 ÷ 2 = 418.8 (2)837.6

98.8 ÷ 0.4 = 247 (4)988.

25.5 ÷ 0.5 = 51 (5)255.

Pages 26-27

1. (10 + 5) x 2 − 20 =
15 x 2 − 20 =
30 − 20 =
10

3. 5^2 − 15 + 4 =
25 − 15 + 4 =
10 + 4 =
14

2. 24 ÷ (12 − 6) =
24 ÷ 6 =
4

4. (24 + 4) ÷ 7 =
28 ÷ 7 =
4

5. $(7 - 3)^2$ − 12 ÷ 2 + 5 x 2 =
16 − 12 ÷ 2 + 5 x 2 =
16 − 6 + 5 x 2 =
16 − 6 + 10 =
10 + 10 = 20

6. 5 x (8 + 4) + 14 ÷ 2 =
5 x 12 + 14 ÷ 2 =
60 + 14 ÷ 2 =
60 + 7 = 67

7. 6^2 + (9 − 3) + 18 ÷ 9 =
6^2 + 6 + 18 ÷ 9 =
36 + 6 + 18 ÷ 9 =
36+6+2=
42 + 2 = 44

8. 10^2 + (25 ÷ 5) − 50 ÷ 5 =
10^2 + 5 − 50 ÷ 5 =
100 + 5 − 50 ÷ 5 =
100 + 5 − 10 =
105 − 10 = 95

1. 18−4x2=10
2. 10+5x3=25
3. 12−9÷3+6=15

Pages 28-29

x	y	Coordinates
1	1	(1, 1)
2	2	(2, 2)
3	3	(3, 3)
4	4	(4, 4)
5	5	(5, 5)
6	6	(6, 6)

Answers

Pages 28-29 cont.

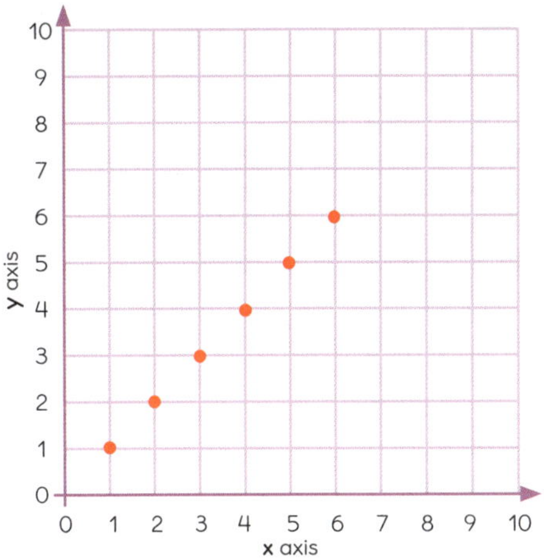

x	y	Coordinates
0	9	(0, 9)
1	8	(1, 8)
2	7	(2, 7)
3	6	(3, 6)
4	5	(4, 5)
5	4	(5, 4)

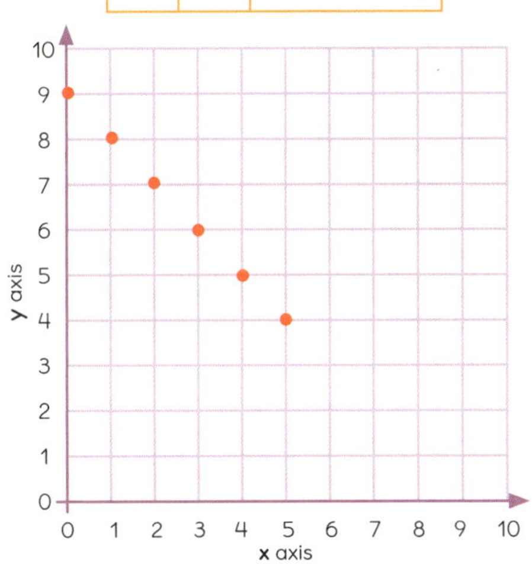

x	y	Coordinates
0	5	(0, 5)
1	5	(1, 5)
2	5	(2, 5)
3	5	(3, 5)
4	5	(4, 5)
5	5	(5, 5)

Pages 28-29 cont.

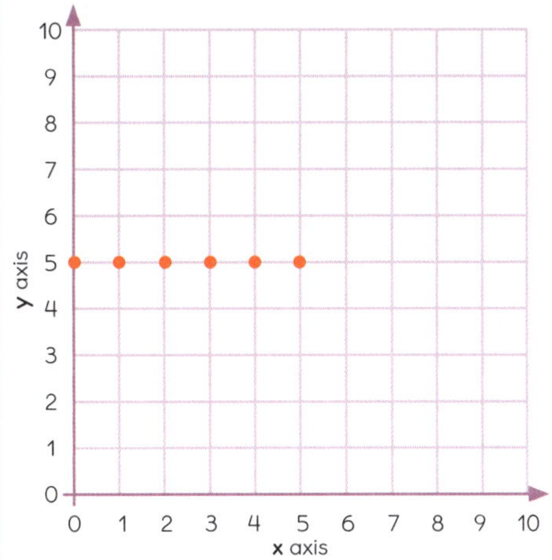

Pages 30-31

$\frac{5}{6} + \frac{3}{4} = \frac{10}{12} + \frac{9}{12} = \frac{19}{12} = 1\frac{7}{12}$

$2\frac{3}{5} + 1\frac{3}{10} = 2\frac{6}{10} + 1\frac{3}{10} = 3\frac{9}{10}$

2. $3\frac{4}{9}$ 3. $4\frac{7}{12}$ 4. $\frac{1}{3}$ 5. $\frac{2}{3}$ 6. $\frac{5}{6}$

Page 33

1. $\frac{5}{8}$ 2. $\frac{1}{12}$ 3. $\frac{1}{12}$ 4. $\frac{1}{8}$

5. $3\frac{5}{8}$ 6. $3\frac{11}{20}$ 7. $4\frac{5}{8}$ 8. $2\frac{1}{8}$

Page 34

$\frac{20}{100} + \frac{2}{100} = \frac{22}{100} = \frac{11}{50}$

$\frac{40}{100} + \frac{5}{100} = \frac{45}{100} = \frac{9}{20}$

Page 35

$\frac{75}{100} - \frac{70}{100} = \frac{5}{100} = \frac{1}{20}$

$\frac{50}{100} - \frac{20}{100} = \frac{30}{100} = \frac{3}{10}$

$\frac{40}{100} - \frac{30}{100} = \frac{10}{100} = \frac{1}{10}$

Pages 36-37

1. $\frac{1}{3} = \frac{4}{12}$ $\frac{1}{4} = \frac{3}{12}$

$\frac{4}{12} + \frac{3}{12} = \frac{7}{12}$ $\frac{12}{12} - \frac{7}{12} = \frac{5}{12}$

$\frac{5}{12}$ are caramel-flavored.

2. $\frac{3}{5} = \frac{9}{15}$ $\frac{1}{3} = \frac{5}{15}$

$\frac{9}{15} + \frac{5}{15} = \frac{14}{15}$ $\frac{15}{15} - \frac{14}{15} = \frac{1}{15}$

$\frac{1}{15}$ of the flour is left.

3. $\frac{2}{3} = \frac{10}{15}$ $\frac{4}{5} = \frac{12}{15}$

$\frac{12}{15} - \frac{10}{15} = \frac{2}{15}$

Walter learned $\frac{2}{15}$ more words.

4. $\frac{3}{4} = \frac{9}{12}$ $\frac{1}{6} = \frac{2}{12}$

$\frac{9}{12} + \frac{2}{12} = \frac{11}{12}$ $\frac{12}{12} - \frac{11}{12} = \frac{1}{12}$

$\frac{1}{12}$ of Nina's homework needs to be completed.

Pages 38-39

$\frac{36}{3} = 12$ They each earn 12 dollars.

1. $\frac{24}{6} = 4$ party favors in each bag.
2. $\frac{64}{8} = 8$ bulbs in each pot.
3. They each have to write $\frac{19}{2} = 9\frac{1}{2}$ pages.
4. They each get $\frac{28}{8} = 3\frac{4}{8} = 3\frac{1}{2}$ sheets.

Pages 40-41

1. $\frac{5}{3} = 1\frac{2}{3}$ 2. $\frac{7}{4} = 1\frac{3}{4}$

3. $\frac{6}{5} = 1\frac{1}{5}$ 4. $\frac{7}{6} = 1\frac{1}{6}$

1. $\frac{8}{3} = 2\frac{2}{3}$ 2. $\frac{6}{4} = 1\frac{1}{2}$

3. $\frac{10}{5} = 2$ 4. $\frac{6}{3} = 2$

Pages 42-43

1. $\frac{4}{1} \times \frac{3}{5} = \frac{12}{5} = 2\frac{2}{5}$
2. $\frac{5}{1} \times \frac{5}{6} = \frac{25}{6} = 4\frac{1}{6}$
3. $\frac{3}{1} \times \frac{3}{4} = \frac{9}{4} = 2\frac{1}{4}$

Answers

Pages 42-43 cont.

4. $\frac{6}{1} \times \frac{5}{8} = \frac{30}{8} = 3\frac{6}{8} = 3\frac{3}{4}$
5. $\frac{7}{1} \times \frac{3}{10} = \frac{21}{10} = 2\frac{1}{10}$
6. $\frac{8}{1} \times \frac{7}{8} = \frac{56}{8} = 7$
7. $\frac{9}{1} \times \frac{5}{12} = \frac{45}{12} = 3\frac{9}{12} = 3\frac{3}{4}$

Pages 44-45

1. $\frac{1}{12}$ 2. $\frac{1}{8}$ 3. $\frac{2}{12} = \frac{1}{6}$ 4. $\frac{3}{10}$

Page 46

Alan eats 6 sections.

Number of sections Alan eats → $\frac{6}{12} = \frac{1}{2}$

Total number of sections in the candy bar →

Check the math: $\frac{6}{12} = \frac{1}{2}$

Page 47

1. < 2. < 3. < 4. <
5. > 6. < 7. > 8. <

Page 49

2. $2\frac{3}{4}$ cups for 4 people

$\frac{1}{2} + \frac{1}{2} + \frac{3}{8} = 1\frac{3}{8}$ cups for 2 people

$\frac{1}{2} \times \frac{11}{4} = \frac{11}{8} = 1\frac{3}{8}$

3. $1\frac{1}{3}$ cups for 3 people

$\frac{1}{3} + \frac{1}{9} = \frac{4}{9}$ cup for 1 person

$\frac{1}{3} \times \frac{4}{3} = \frac{4}{9}$

Pages 50-51

1. Each child gets $\frac{1}{12}$ of the whole sheet of stickers.

$\frac{1}{12} \times 4 - \frac{1}{3}$

2. $\frac{1}{2} \div 3 = \frac{1}{6}$

Each child gets $\frac{1}{6}$ of the pencils in the box.

$\frac{1}{6} \times 3 = \frac{1}{2}$

3. $\frac{1}{4} \div 2 = \frac{1}{8}$

We each get $\frac{1}{8}$ of the whole pizza.

$\frac{1}{8} \times 2 = \frac{1}{4}$

4. $\frac{1}{3} \div 3 = \frac{1}{9}$

Each dog gets $\frac{1}{9}$ of all the biscuits in the box.

$\frac{1}{9} \times 3 = \frac{1}{3}$

Pages 52-53

1. $20 \times \frac{1}{5} = 4$
2. $3 \div \frac{1}{8} = 24$ $24 \times \frac{1}{8} = 3$
3. $3 \div \frac{1}{6} = 18$ $18 \times \frac{1}{6} = 3$
4. $4 \div \frac{1}{4} = 16$ $16 \times \frac{1}{4} = 4$

Pages 54-55

1. Each child gets $\frac{1}{4}$ of one dollar.

$100 \div 4 = 25¢$, $\frac{100}{4} = 25¢$.

$\frac{1}{4}$ of \$1 is worth 25¢ $25 \times 4 = 100$

2. $\frac{1}{5}$ Each child gets $\frac{1}{5}$ of one dollar.

$100 \div 5 = 20¢$, $\frac{100}{5} = 20¢$.

$\frac{1}{5}$ of \$1 is worth 20¢ $20 \times 5 = 100$

3. $\frac{3 \times 20}{5 \times 20} = \frac{60}{100}$ 60 hundredths = 60¢

4. $\frac{1}{4} = \frac{25}{100} = 25¢$ $\frac{3}{4} = \frac{75}{100} = 75¢$

$75 \times 2 = 150¢$

Page 56

2. \$0.60 3. \$0.90 4. \$2.30
5. \$2.20 6. \$0.27 7. \$0.53
8. \$10.05 9. \$3.03 10. \$0.99

Page 57

2. $5¢ = \frac{5}{100} = \frac{1}{20}$ 3. $10¢ = \frac{10}{100} = \frac{1}{10}$
4. $25¢ = \frac{25}{100} = \frac{1}{4}$

1. $20¢ = \frac{20}{100} = \frac{1}{5}$ 2. $50¢ = \frac{50}{100} = \frac{1}{2}$
3. $60¢ = \frac{60}{100} = \frac{6}{10} = \frac{3}{5}$
4. $75¢ = \frac{75}{100} = \frac{3}{4}$
5. $80¢ = \frac{80}{100} = \frac{4}{5}$

Page 58

Money Total	As a Fraction	As a Decimal Price
	$\frac{5}{100}$	\$0.05
	$\frac{75}{100}$	\$0.75
	$1\frac{25}{100}$	\$1.25
	$\frac{39}{100}$	\$0.39
	$2\frac{15}{100}$	\$2.15

Page 59

1. 3.1 2. 4.5 3. 9.7 4. 8.6
5. 2.05 6. 3.01 7. 9.50 8. 10.20
9. 2.001 10. 3.002 11. 3.015 12. 6.025

Page 60

1. 10 $10\overline{)9.0}$ = 0.9
3. 4 $4\overline{)1.00}$ = 0.25
2. 4 $4\overline{)3.00}$ = 0.75
4. 2 $2\overline{)1.0}$ = 0.5

Answers

Page 61

1. $\frac{3}{8} = 3 \div 8$

$$\begin{array}{r} 0.375 \\ 8\overline{)3.000} \\ -\ 24\ \\ \hline 60 \\ -\ 56\ \\ \hline 40 \\ -\ 40 \\ \hline 00 \end{array}$$

2.

$$\begin{array}{r} 0.625 \\ 8\overline{)5.000} \\ -\ 48\ \\ \hline 20 \\ -\ 16\ \\ \hline 40 \\ -\ 40 \\ \hline 00 \end{array}$$

$\frac{5}{8} = 0.625$

3.

$$\begin{array}{r} 0.875 \\ 8\overline{)7.000} \\ -\ 64\ \\ \hline 60 \\ -\ 56\ \\ \hline 40 \\ -\ 40 \\ \hline 00 \end{array}$$

$\frac{7}{8} = 0.875$

Page 62

1. 72 in.
2. 4 ft.
3. 5 ft., 60 ÷ 12 = 5
4. 120 in., 10 x 12 = 120
5. 45 ft., 15 x 3 = 45
6. 33 yd., 99 ÷ 3 = 33

Page 63

1. 2 ft. 2. 108 in. 3. 28 ft. 4. 940 yd.

Page 64

3. 600 cm 4. 165 mm
5. 600 m 6. 6 km

Page 65

1. 23 cm 2. 40 cm 3. 0.4 km

Page 66

1. 1 lb. 4 oz. 2. 192 oz.
3. 800 oz., 50 x 16 = 800
4. 6 lb., 96 ÷ 16 = 6
5. 12,000 lb., 6 x 2,000 = 12,000
6. 4 tn., 8,000 ÷ 2,000 = 4
7. 14 lb., 224 ÷ 16 = 14
8. 50,000 lb., 25 x 2,000 = 50,000

Page 67

1. 9 tn.
2. A baby elephant is 27 times heavier. A human baby is 32 times heavier.
3. a) 1 tn. b) 4,800 oz.

Page 68

3. 5 kg 4. 7,000 g
5. 6,000 g 6. 4 kg
7. 5,500 g 8. 3.5 kg

Page 69

1. 2.7 kg
2. 3 pineapples = 3,000 g
4 watermelons = 4,800 g
2 bunches of bananas = 1,000 g
total weight = 8,800 g
3. 8 apples = 1.2 kg
4. 10 oranges

Page 70

1. 24 pt. 2. 12 c. 3. 40 qt.
4. 4 pt. 5. 2 gal. 6. 4 gal.

Page 71

1. 24 players can have 1 cup each.
12 players can have 2 cups each.
2. 15 qt.
3. 848 c.
4. 8 gal.

Page 72

Quantity in mL	Quantity in L	As a Fraction
100 mL	0.10 L	$\frac{1}{10}$ L
200 mL	0.20 L	$\frac{2}{10}$ or $\frac{1}{5}$ L
300 mL	0.30 L	$\frac{3}{10}$ L
400 mL	0.40 L	$\frac{4}{10}$ or $\frac{2}{5}$ L
800 mL	0.80 L	$\frac{8}{10}$ or $\frac{4}{5}$ L
1,100 mL	1.10 L	$1\frac{1}{10}$ L

Page 73

1. 4 pitchers 2. 2,800 mL
3. 900 mL is < a liter 4. 200 mL

Page 74

1. 60 x 60 = 3,600

$$\begin{array}{r} \text{T U} \\ 6\ 0 \\ \times\ \ 6\ 0 \\ \hline 0\ 0 \\ 3,\ 6\ 0\ 0 \\ \hline 3,\ 6\ 0\ 0 \end{array}$$

2. 60 x 24 = 1,440

$$\begin{array}{r} \text{T U} \\ 6\ 0 \\ \times\ \ 2\ 4 \\ \hline 2\ 4\ 0 \\ 1,\ 2\ 0\ 0 \\ \hline 1,\ 4\ 4\ 0 \end{array}$$

3. 24 x 365 = 8,760

	300	60	5
20	6,000	1,200	100
4	1,200	240	20

6000 + 1,200 + 100 + 1,200 + 240 + 20 = 8,760

Page 75

1. Step 1: 10:40 a.m.
Step 2: 11:00 a.m.
Step 3: 11:30 a.m.
He arrived home at 11:30 a.m.
2. Step 1: 3:30 p.m.
Step 2: 3:00 p.m.
Step 3: 2:50 p.m.
The party started at 2:50 p.m.

Pages 76-77

1. 4 in. 2. 2 days
3. 3 days 4. 21 in.

7 + 6 + 8 = 21

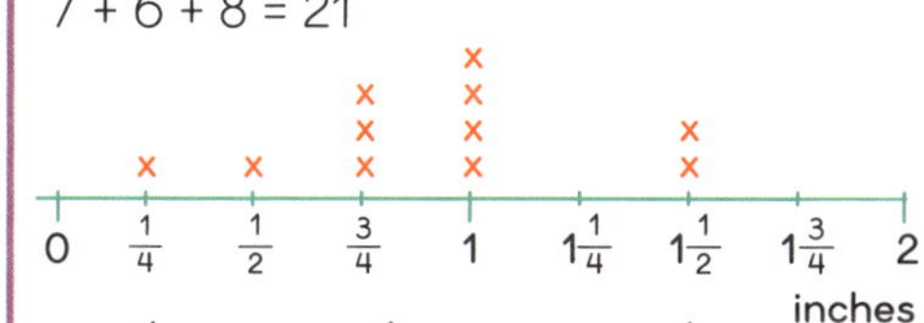

1. $1\frac{1}{2}$ in. 2. $\frac{1}{4}$ in. 3. $1\frac{1}{4}$ in.
4. 10 in. $\frac{3}{4} + 2\frac{1}{4} + 4 + 3 = 10$
5. 5 in.

Pages 78-79

1. n = 45° 2. n = 22° acute
3. n = 30° acute 4. n = 136° obtuse
5. n = 23° acute 6. n = 80° acute
7. n = 90° right 8. n = 50° acute
9. n = 135° obtuse
10. n = 55° acute, m = 125° obtuse

Answers

Page 80

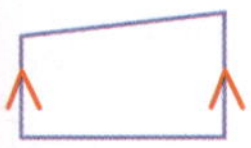
trapezoid

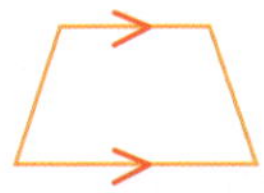
trapezoid

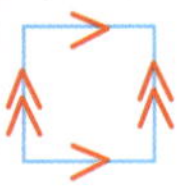
square

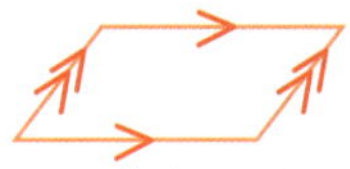
parallelogram

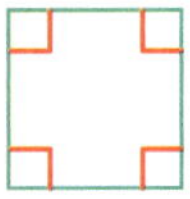
square

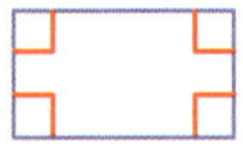
rectangle

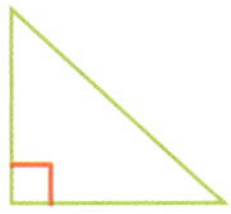
right triangle

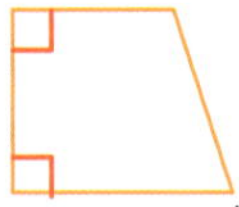
trapezoid

Page 81

1. True 2. False 3. False 4. True

1. A parallelogram has 2 pairs of parallel sides.
2. A square has 4 sides the same length and 4 right angles.

Pages 82-83

quadrilaterals

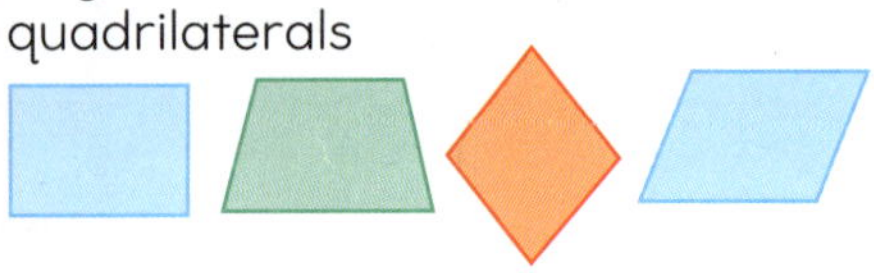

trapezoids

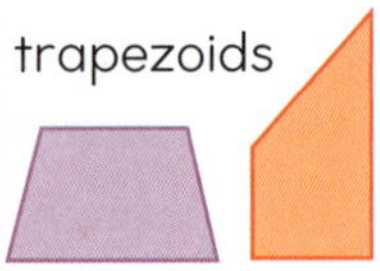

parallelograms

rhombuses

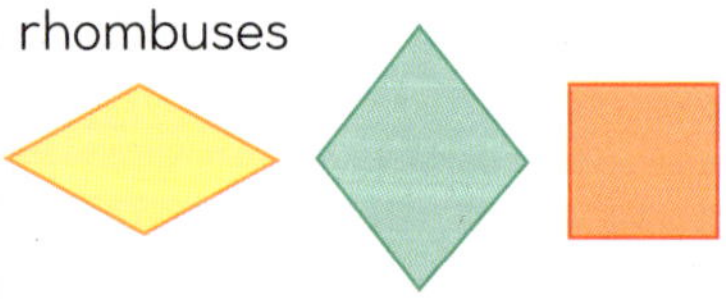

rectangles

square

Pages 84-85

20 + 6 + 20 + 22 + 40 + 16 = 124 in.

1. a = 18 — 8 a = 10
   b = 40 + 22 b = 62
   40 + 8 + 22 + 10 + 62 + 18 = 160 yd.
2. a = 66 — 22 a = 44
   b = 55 — 30 b = 25
   66 + 55 + 22 + 25 + 44 + 30 = 242 ft.

12 x 6 = 72 cm 50 x 5 = 250 m
8 x 20 = 160 m
a = 7
7 + b + a + b = 42 in.
14 + b + b = 42 in.
42 — 14 = 28 in.
b + b = 28 in.
b = 14 in.

Pages 86-87

Shape A: Volume = 9 + 9 + 9
= 27 cubic units.
Shape B: Volume = 8 x 2
= 16 cubic units.
1. V = 20 x 10 x 20
= 4,000 cubic inches.
2. V= 5 x 5 x 15
= 375 cubic centimeters.
3. V = 20 x 8 x 8 = 1,280 cubic feet.

Pages 88-89

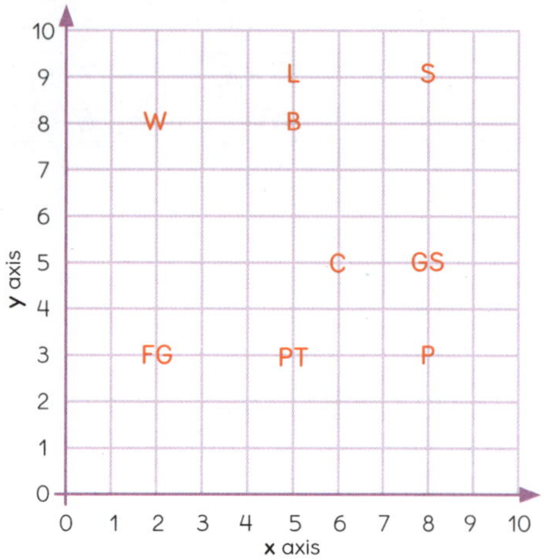

1. a) 100 yards, b) 500 yards,
   c) 600 yards, d) 400 yards.
2. The picnic tables are halfway between them.
3. The lake is closer to the sculpture.
4. The sculpture is farther away from the gift shop.
5. 200 yards

Page 90

1. 108 ÷ 12 = 9 n = 9 ft.
Perimeter = 12 + 9 + 12 + 9 ft. = 42 ft.
2. Area of the path = 6 x 3 = 18 ft.^{2}
Area of the patio = 6 x 6 = 36 ft.^{2}
Total area of the path and patio
= 18 + 36 = 54 ft.^{2}
3. 9 tiles